*Samuel French Acting Edition*

P9-BVG-672

# Rhinoceros

*by* Eugène Ionesco

*Translated by* Derek Prouse

SAMUELFRENCH.COM    SAMUELFRENCH.CO.UK

**FOR PRODUCTION ENQUIRIES**

UNITED STATES AND CANADA
Info@SamuelFrench.com
1-866-598-8449

UNITED KINGDOM AND EUROPE
Plays@SamuelFrench.co.uk
020-7255-4302

Each title is subject to availability from Samuel French, depending upon country of performance. Please be aware that *RHINOCEROS* may not be licensed by Samuel French in your territory. Professional and amateur producers should contact the nearest Samuel French office or licensing partner to verify availability.

For all enquiries regarding motion picture, television, and other media rights, please contact Samuel French.

## MUSIC USE NOTE

Licensees are solely responsible for obtaining formal written permission from copyright owners to use copyrighted music in the performance of this play and are strongly cautioned to do so. If no such permission is obtained by the licensee, then the licensee must use only original music that the licensee owns and controls. Licensees are solely responsible and liable for all music clearances and shall indemnify the copyright owners of the play(s) and their licensing agent, Samuel French, against any costs, expenses, losses and liabilities arising from the use of music by licensees. Please contact the appropriate music licensing authority in your territory for the rights to any incidental music.

## IMPORTANT BILLING AND CREDIT REQUIREMENTS

If you have obtained performance rights to this title, please refer to your licensing agreement for important billing and credit requirements.

*RHINOCEROS* was first produced by the Old Vic Company at the Theatre Royal, Bristol, England on the 5th September 1960. It was directed by John Hale with designs by Jane Graham. The cast was as follows:

**THE WAITRESS**. . . . . . . . . . . . . . . . . . . . . . . . . . . . . . . . . . . . . . . . . . . . Claire Pollock

**THE GROCER'S WIFE** . . . . . . . . . . . . . . . . . . . . . . . . . . . . . . . . . . Stephanie Cole

**THE HOUSEWIFE**. . . . . . . . . . . . . . . . . . . . . . . . . . . . . . . . . . . . Josephine Tewson

**BERENGER**. . . . . . . . . . . . . . . . . . . . . . . . . . . . . . . . . . . . . . . . . . . . . . Richard Gale

**JEAN**. . . . . . . . . . . . . . . . . . . . . . . . . . . . . . . . . . . . . . . . . . . . . Michael Mellinger

**THE GROCER**. . . . . . . . . . . . . . . . . . . . . . . . . . . . . . . . . . . . . . . . . . Terence Davies

**THE OLD GENTLEMAN**. . . . . . . . . . . . . . . . . . . . . . . . . . . . . . . . . Norman Tyrrell

**THE LOGICIAN** . . . . . . . . . . . . . . . . . . . . . . . . . . . . . . . . . . . . . . Leonard Rossiter

**THE CAFÉ PROPRIETOR** . . . . . . . . . . . . . . . . . . . . . . . . . . . . . . . Michael Lynch

**DAISY** . . . . . . . . . . . . . . . . . . . . . . . . . . . . . . . . . . . . . . . . . . . . . . Annette Crosbie

**DUDARD**. . . . . . . . . . . . . . . . . . . . . . . . . . . . . . . . . . . . . . . . . . . . . . . Peter Birrel

**BOTARD** . . . . . . . . . . . . . . . . . . . . . . . . . . . . . . . . . . . . . . . . . . . . . . Ewan Hooper

**MR. PAPILLON**. . . . . . . . . . . . . . . . . . . . . . . . . . . . . . . . . . . . . . Michael Kilgarriff

**MRS. BŒUF**. . . . . . . . . . . . . . . . . . . . . . . . . . . . . . . . . . . . . . . . . . Margaret Jones

**A FIREMAN** . . . . . . . . . . . . . . . . . . . . . . . . . . . . . . . . . . . . . . . . . . . Robin Phillips

# CHARACTERS
**THE WAITRESS**
**THE GROCER'S WIFE**
**THE HOUSEWIFE**
**BERENGER**
**JEAN**
**THE GROCER**
**THE OLD GENTLEMAN**
**THE LOGICIAN**
**THE CAFÉ PROPRIETOR**
**DAISY**
**DUDARD**
**BOTARD**
**MR. PAPILLON**
**MRS. BŒUF**
**A FIREMAN**

# SETTING
### Act I
**Scene One**: A square in a small French provincial town.
**Scene Two**: The office of a firm of law publications.

### Act II
Jean's room.

### Act III
Berenger's room.

# TIME
The present.

### Act I
**Scene One**: Midday on a Sunday in summer.
**Scene Two**: The following morning.

### Act II
The afternoon of the same day.

### Act III
A few days later.

# ACT I

## Scene One

*(House lights fade.)*

*(Cue No. 01: Church bells, etc.)*

*(SCENE: A square in a small French provincial town. Midday on a Sunday in summer, upstage left center is the* **GROCER**'s *house, ground floor and one storey. On the ground floor there is the shop window with the glass-panelled door left of it. The word "Épicerie" is written in bold letters above the shop window. The two windows on the first floor are the living room of the* **GROCER** *and his* **WIFE**. *The upstage window is practical and there is access to it inside the house, upstage center, there is a little street in perspective. Slightly at an angle right is the entrance to the café. There is one storey with a window over the café. In front of the café, over the tables, is a striped awning. A typical French "pissoir" is center. Two dusty trees are upstage right and left. There is an expanse of blue sky, the light is harsh and the buildings have very white walls. Two café tables, each with chairs upstage right and upstage left of them, stand left center and downstage right center. A third table, with a potted plant, stands at the downstage side of the café entrance, and*

*two small tables are inside the entrance. A menu board leans against the table right.)*

*(AT RISE: The **WAITRESS** is at the table right center, adjusting the cloth. She takes an ashtray from the chair upstage left of the table and puts it on the center of the table. The **GROCER'S WIFE** is at the door of her shop, sweeping the floor. After a moment, the **HOUSEWIFE** enters upstage right, carrying a basket of provisions on one arm and a cat under the other. She is about to go upstage left, sees the **GROCER'S WIFE**, turns downstage, crosses and exits downstage left.)*

**GROCER'S WIFE.** Oh, that woman gets on my nerves. *(Over her shoulder to her husband in the shop.)* Too stuck-up to buy from us nowadays.

*(The **GROCER'S WIFE** exits to the shop. The **WAITRESS** exits to the café. **BERENGER** enters downstage left. He is unshaven and hatless, is without his tie, and has unkempt hair and creased clothes; everything about him indicates negligence. He seems weary and half-asleep and yawns from time to time. **JEAN** enters upstage right. He is very fastidiously dressed in a brown suit, red tie, stiff collar, and a brown hat. He has a reddish face. His shoes are yellow and well polished. He wears gloves and carries a cane.)*

*(Fade sound.)*

**JEAN.** *(Crossing briskly to center.)* Oh, so you managed to get here at last, Berenger.

**BERENGER.** *(Wandering to left of **JEAN**; looking off left over his left shoulder.)* Morning, Jean.

**JEAN.** Late as usual, of course.

*(He looks at his wrist watch.)*

Our appointment was for eleven-thirty. And now it's practically midday.

**BERENGER**. I'm sorry. Have you been waiting long?

**JEAN**. *(Removing his gloves.)* No, I've only just arrived myself, as you saw.

**BERENGER**. In that case I don't feel so bad, if you've only just...

**JEAN**. *(Crossing to the table right center.)* It's different with me.

> *(He flicks the dust from the chair upstage right of the table with his gloves and sits.)*

I don't like waiting; I've no time to waste. And as you're never on time, I come late on purpose – at a time when I presume you'll be there.

> *(He taps the chair upstage left of the table with his cane for* **BERENGER** *to sit.)*

**BERENGER**. *(Crossing to the table right center.)* You're right – quite right, but...

**JEAN**. Now don't try to pretend you're ever on time.

**BERENGER**. *(Sitting upstage left of the table right center.)* No, of course not – I wouldn't say that.

**JEAN**. There you are, you see!

**BERENGER**. What are you drinking?

**JEAN**. You mean to say you've got a thirst even at this time in the morning?

**BERENGER**. It's so hot and dry.

**JEAN**. The more you drink the thirstier you get – popular science tells us that...

**BERENGER** *(Scratching his stomach.)* It would be less dry, and we'd be less thirsty, if they'd invent us some scientific clouds in the sky.

**JEAN**. *(Studying* **BERENGER** *closely.)* That wouldn't help you any. You're not thirsty for water, Berenger.

**BERENGER**. I don't understand what you mean.

**JEAN**. You know perfectly well what I mean. I'm talking about your parched throat. That's a territory that can't get enough.

*(He laughs loudly.)*

**BERENGER**. To compare my throat to a piece of land seems –

**JEAN**. *(Interrupting.)* You're in a bad way, my friend.

**BERENGER**. In a bad way? You think so?

**JEAN**. I'm not blind, you know. You're dropping with fatigue. You've gone without your sleep again, you yawn all the time, you're dead tired...

**BERENGER**. My head feels a bit thick.

**JEAN**. You reek of alcohol.

**BERENGER**. I have got a bit of a hangover, it's true.

**JEAN**. It's the same every Sunday morning – not to mention the other days of the week.

**BERENGER**. Oh, no, it's less frequent during the week, because of the office.

**JEAN**. And what's happened to your tie? Lost it during your orgy, I suppose.

**BERENGER**. *(Putting his hand to his neck.)* You're right. That's funny. Whatever could I have done with it?

**JEAN**. *(Taking a tie from his pocket.)* Here, put this one on.

*(He hands the tie to **BERENGER**.)*

**BERENGER**. Oh, thank you, that is kind.

*(He fiddles with the tie.)*

**JEAN**. Your hair's all over the place.

*(**BERENGER** runs his fingers through his hair.
**JEAN** takes a pocket comb and mirror from
his pocket.)*

Here – here's a comb.

**BERENGER**. *(Taking the comb.)* Thank you.

*(He vaguely combs his hair.)*

**JEAN**. You haven't even shaved. Just take a look at yourself.

*(He hands the mirror to **BERENGER**.)*

**BERENGER.** *(He looks at himself in the mirror, then puts out his tongue and examines it.)* My tongue's all coated.

*(He returns the comb to* **JEAN**.*)*

**JEAN.** I'm not surprised.

*(He pockets the comb.)*

You're heading for cirrhosis, my friend.

*(***BERENGER**, *still looking in the mirror, holds out the tie which* **JEAN** *takes.)*

**BERENGER.** *(Worried.)* Do you think so?

**JEAN.** *(Taking the mirror from* **BERENGER**.*)* Keep the tie, I've got plenty more.

*(He returns the tie to* **BERENGER**, *looks admiringly at himself in the mirror, then puts it in his pocket.)*

*(***BERENGER** *puts the tie around his neck, fiddles with it, but does not succeed in fixing it.)*

**BERENGER.** *(After a pause; admiringly.)* You always look so immaculate.

**JEAN.** *(Continuing his inspection of* **BERENGER**.*)* Your clothes are all crumpled, they're a disgrace. Your shirt is downright filthy, and your shoes...

*(He rises, stands above the table and leans over it.* **BERENGER** *tries to hide his feet under the table.)*

Your shoes haven't been touched. What a mess you're in. And look at your shoulders...

**BERENGER.** *(Facing front and putting his hands to his shoulders.)* What's the matter with my shoulders?

**JEAN.** Turn round. Come on, turn round.

*(***BERENGER** *turns his back on* **JEAN**.*)*

You've been leaning against some wall.

*(***BERENGER** *holds his hand out docilely to* **JEAN**.*)*

**JEAN.** No, I haven't got a brush with me; it would make my pockets bulge.

> (**BERENGER**, *still docile, flicks his shoulders to get rid of the white dust.* **JEAN** *crosses above* **BERENGER** *and stands below the table left center.*)

Heavens! Where did you get all that from?

**BERENGER.** I don't remember.

**JEAN.** It's a positive disgrace! I feel ashamed to be your friend.

**BERENGER.** You're very hard on me.

**JEAN.** I've every reason to be.

**BERENGER.** Listen, Jean. There are so few distractions in this town – I get so bored. I'm not made for the work I'm doing – every day at the office, eight hours a day – and only three weeks' holiday a year. When Saturday night comes round I feel exhausted and so – you know how it is – just to relax...

**JEAN.** My dear man, everybody has to work. I spend eight hours a day in the office the same as everyone else. And I only get three weeks off a year, but even so you don't catch me...

> (*He mimes a splendid golf stroke with his cane.*)

Willpower, my good man!

**BERENGER.** But everybody hasn't got as much willpower as you have. I can't get used to it. I just can't get used to life.

**JEAN.** Everybody has to get used to it.

> (*He moves to left of* **BERENGER.**)

Or do you consider yourself some superior being?

**BERENGER.** I don't pretend to be...

**JEAN.** (*Interrupting.*) I'm just as good as you are; I think with all due modesty I may say I'm better.

> (*He emphasizes by tapping.*)

The superior man is the man who fulfills his duty.

**BERENGER**. What duty?

**JEAN**. His duty – his duty as an employee, for example.

> *(He moves above the table right center.)*

**BERENGER**. *(Fixing his tie.)* Oh, yes, his duty as an employee.

> *(He gives a loud belch.)*

**JEAN**. Where did your debauch take place last night?

> *(He sits right of the table right center.)*

If you can remember.

**BERENGER**. We were celebrating Auguste's birthday, our friend Auguste –

**JEAN**. Our friend Auguste? Nobody invited me to our friend Auguste's birthday.

> *(Cue No. 02: Rhino charge.)*

> *(At this moment a noise is heard, far off, but swiftly approaching, of a beast panting in its headlong course, and of a long trumpeting.)*

**BERENGER**. I couldn't refuse. It wouldn't have been nice.

**JEAN**. Did I go there?

**BERENGER**. Well, perhaps it was because you weren't invited.

> *(The **WAITRESS** enters from the café and stands above the table right center between **JEAN** and **BERENGER**.)*

**WAITRESS**. Good morning, gentlemen. Can I get you something to drink?

> *(The noise becomes very loud.)*

**JEAN**. *(To **BERENGER**; almost shouting to make himself heard above the noise of which he has not become conscious.)* True, I was not invited. That honour was denied me. But in any case, I can assure you, that even if I had been invited, I would not have gone, because –

> *(The noise becomes intense.)*

**JEAN.** What's going on?

> *(The noise of a powerful, heavy animal, galloping at great speed, and panting, is heard very close.)*

Whatever is it?

**WAITRESS.** Whatever is it?

> *(**BERENGER,** still listless and without appearing to hear anything at all, replies tranquilly to **JEAN** about the invitation; his lips move but one does not hear what he says. The following episode must be played very fast, each repeating in swift succession, "Oh, a rhinoceros." **JEAN** bounds to his feet, knocking his chair over as he does so, looks off left and points, whilst **BERENGER,** still a little dopey, remains seated.)*

**JEAN.** Oh, a rhinoceros!

> *(The noise made by the animal dies away swiftly and one can already hear the following words. The **GROCER'S WIFE** enters from the shop, leaving the door open, moves left center and looks offstage left.)*

**WAITRESS.** *(Looking offstage left.)* Oh, a rhinoceros!

**GROCER'S WIFE.** Oh, a rhinoceros! *(She calls into the shop.)* Quick, come and look; it's a rhinoceros!

> *(They are all looking off left, after the animal.)*

**JEAN.** *(Crossing down left and looking off.)* It's rushing straight ahead, brushing up against the shop windows.

> *(The **GROCER** enters from the shop and looks off left.)*

**WAITRESS.** *(Putting her hands on her hips.)* Well!

**GROCER.** Oh, a rhinoceros!

**HOUSEWIFE.** *(Offstage left.)* Oh!

*(The **LOGICIAN** enters quickly up right and crosses to left of the **WAITRESS**. He has a little grey moustache and an eyeglass and is wearing a straw hat.)*

**LOGICIAN**. *(Looking offstage left.)* A rhinoceros going full-tilt on the opposite pavement.

*(Sound loud.)*

*(The **HOUSEWIFE** runs on left, carrying her basket and cat.)*

*(Sound fading slowly.)*

*(The **OLD GENTLEMAN** runs on down left. He is elegantly dressed, with white spats, a soft hat and an ivory-handled cane. The **HOUSEWIFE**, as she runs left center, bumps into the **OLD GENTLEMAN** and drops her basket. The contents scatter over the ground, but she does not drop her cat. The **OLD GENTLEMAN** bumps from the **HOUSEWIFE** into the **GROCER** and his **WIFE**. Cries of "oh" and "ah" and the sounds of people running are heard offstage left.)*

**HOUSEWIFE**. Ah! Oh!

*(She sits right of the table left center and strokes the cat.)*

*(The **CAFÉ PROPRIETOR** enters from the café and moves to right of the **WAITRESS**. **BERENGER** remains apathetically seated.)*

**PROPRIETOR**. What's going on?

**OLD GENTLEMAN**. *(To the **GROCER** and his **WIFE**.)* Excuse me, please.

**GROCER'S WIFE**. *(Jostled and jostling her **HUSBAND**; to the **OLD GENTLEMAN**.)* Watch out with that stick!

**GROCER**. Look where you're going, can't you!

**PROPRIETOR**. What's going on?

**WAITRESS**. *(To the **PROPRIETOR**.)* A rhinoceros!

**PROPRIETOR.** You're seeing things.

>   *(He looks offstage left.)*

Well, I'll be...!

**HOUSEWIFE.** Ah!

>   *(She soothes the cat.)*

There, they frightened the poor pussy.

>   *(Sound out.)*

>   *(The noises fade.)*

**PROPRIETOR.** Well, of all things.

>   *(He picks up the fallen chair and puts it right of the table right center.)*

**JEAN.** Well, of all things!

**HOUSEWIFE.** Well, of all things!

**GROCER, GROCER'S WIFE & OLD GENTLEMAN.** Well, of all things!

**JEAN.** Well, of all things! *(To* **BERENGER.***)* Did you see that?

**ALL.** *(Except* **BERENGER***; together.)* Well, of all things.

>   *(***JEAN*** exits down left.)*

**BERENGER.** It certainly looked as if it was a rhinoceros. It made plenty of dust.

>   *(He takes out his handkerchief and blows his nose.)*

**HOUSEWIFE.** Well, of all things! Gave me such a scare.

**GROCER.** *(With a step towards the* **HOUSEWIFE.***)* Your basket – and all your things.

>   *(The* **OLD GENTLEMAN** *moves above the table left center and gallantly raises his hat to the* **HOUSEWIFE.** *The* **GROCER'S WIFE** *crosses to right of the* **GROCER.***)*

**PROPRIETOR.** Really, these days, you never know...

**WAITRESS.** Fancy that!

**OLD GENTLEMAN**. *(To the* **HOUSEWIFE**.*)* May I help you pick up your things?

**HOUSEWIFE**. Thank you, how very kind.

> *(The* **OLD GENTLEMAN** *leers at the* **HOUSEWIFE**.*)*

Do put on your hat. Oh, it gave me such a scare.

**LOGICIAN**. Fear is an irrational thing. It must yield to reason.

**WAITRESS**. It's already out of sight.

**OLD GENTLEMAN**. *(To the* **HOUSEWIFE** *and indicating the* **LOGICIAN**.*)* My friend is a logician.

> *(He moves below the table left center and during the following speeches, collects the scattered goods and puts them in the basket.)*

> *(***JEAN** *enters downstage left the* **HOUSEWIFE** *rises.)*

**JEAN**. *(Speaking across to* **BERENGER**.*)* Well, what did you think of that?

**WAITRESS**. Those animals can certainly travel.

**HOUSEWIFE**. *(Shaking hands with the* **LOGICIAN**.*)* Very happy to meet you.

**GROCER'S WIFE**. *(To the* **GROCER**.*)* That'll teach her to buy her things from somebody else.

**JEAN**. *(To the* **PROPRIETOR** *and the* **WAITRESS**.*)* What did you think of that?

**HOUSEWIFE**. *(To the* **LOGICIAN**.*)* I still didn't let my cat go.

**PROPRIETOR**. *(Shrugging.)* You don't often see that.

**HOUSEWIFE**. *(Holding out the cat to the* **LOGICIAN**.*)* Would you hold him a moment?

**WAITRESS**. *(To* **JEAN**.*)* First time I've seen that!

> *(The* **LOGICIAN** *removes his straw hat and takes the cat in it.)*

**LOGICIAN**. It's not spiteful, is it?

**PROPRIETOR**. *(To* **JEAN**.*)* Went past like a rocket.

**HOUSEWIFE**. *(To the* **LOGICIAN**.*)* He wouldn't hurt a fly.

*(She turns to the* **GROCER**.*)*

**HOUSEWIFE**. What happened to my wine?

**GROCER**. *(Crossing to right of his* **WIFE**.*)* I've got plenty more.

**JEAN**. Well, Berenger, what did you think of that?

**GROCER**. *(To the* **HOUSEWIFE**.*)* And good stuff, too.

**PROPRIETOR**. *(To the* **WAITRESS**.*)* Don't hang about.

*(He indicates* **BERENGER** *and* **JEAN**.*)*

Look after these gentlemen.

*(The* **PROPRIETOR** *exits to the café.)*

**BERENGER**. *(To* **JEAN**.*)* What did I think of what?

**GROCER'S WIFE**. *(To the* **GROCER**.*)* Go and get her another bottle.

**JEAN**. *(To* **BERENGER**.*)* Of the rhinoceros, of course. What did you think I meant?

**GROCER**. *(To the* **HOUSEWIFE**.*)* I've got some first-class wine, in unbreakable bottles.

*(The* **GROCER** *exits to the shop.)*

**LOGICIAN**. *(Stroking the cat.)* Puss, puss, puss.

**WAITRESS**. *(Moving to right of* **BERENGER**.*)* What are you drinking?

**BERENGER**. Cognac.

**WAITRESS**. Two cognac – right.

*(She goes to the café entrance.)*

**HOUSEWIFE**. *(Moving to the* **OLD GENTLEMAN** *downstage left.)* Very kind of you, I'm sure.

**WAITRESS**. Two cognac.

*(The* **WAITRESS** *exits to the café.)*

**OLD GENTLEMAN**. *(To the* **HOUSEWIFE**.*)* Oh, please don't mention it, it's a pleasure.

*(The* **GROCER'S WIFE** *exits to the shop. The* **HOUSEWIFE** *puts the basket on the table left*

*center and sorts out the contents, putting some leeks on the top.)*

**LOGICIAN**. Replace them in an orderly fashion.

**JEAN**. *(Crossing and sitting right of the table right center; to **BERENGER**.)* Well, what did you think about it?

**BERENGER**. *(Not knowing what to say.)* Well – nothing – it made a lot of dust.

*(The **GROCER** enters from the shop with a bottle of wine and crosses to the table left center.)*

**GROCER**. *(Seeing the leeks; ironically to the **HOUSEWIFE**.)* I've some good leeks, as well.

**LOGICIAN**. *(Stroking the cat.)* Puss, puss, puss.

**GROCER**. *(Putting the bottle in the basket.)* It's a hundred francs a litre.

*(The **HOUSEWIFE** takes a hundred franc note from her pocket and pays the **GROCER**.)*

**HOUSEWIFE**. *(Crossing to the **OLD GENTLEMAN**.)* Oh, you are kind. Such a pleasure to come across the old French courtesy. Not like the young people today.

**GROCER**. *(Crossing to the shop door.)* You should buy from me. You wouldn't even have to cross the street, and you wouldn't run the risk of these accidents.

*(The **GROCER** exits to the shop.)*

**JEAN**. *(Still thinking of the rhinoceros; to **BERENGER**.)* But you must admit it's extraordinary.

**OLD GENTLEMAN**. *(He raises his hat and kisses the **HOUSEWIFE**'s hand.)* It was a great pleasure to meet you.

**HOUSEWIFE**. *(Crossing to the **LOGICIAN**.)* Thank you very much for holding my cat.

*(She takes the cat from him.)*

**WAITRESS**. *(Enters from the café carrying a tray with two cognacs; putting the drinks on the table right center.)* Two cognacs.

JEAN. *(To* BERENGER.*)* You're incorrigible!

>   *(The* HOUSEWIFE *picks up her basket and crosses to left. The* WAITRESS *exits to the café.)*

OLD GENTLEMAN. *(To the* HOUSEWIFE.*)* May I accompany you part of the way?

BERENGER. *(To* JEAN.*)* I asked for mineral water. She's made a mistake.

>   *(*JEAN, *scornful and disbelieving, shrugs his shoulders.)*

HOUSEWIFE. *(To the* OLD GENTLEMAN.*)* My husband's waiting for me, thank you. Perhaps some other time...

OLD GENTLEMAN. I sincerely hope so, madame.

HOUSEWIFE. So do I.

>   *(The* HOUSEWIFE *gives the* OLD GENTLEMAN *a sweet look and exits left. The* OLD GENTLEMAN *follows her for a step or two. The* LOGICIAN *moves below the table left center.)*

BERENGER. The dust's settled.

>   *(*JEAN *shrugs his shoulders.)*

OLD GENTLEMAN. *(Turning to the* LOGICIAN.*)* Delightful creature.

JEAN. *(To* BERENGER.*)* A rhinoceros! I can't get over it.

OLD GENTLEMAN. *(After casting a last fond look off left.)* Charming, isn't she?

LOGICIAN. *(Moving to right of the* OLD GENTLEMAN.*)* I'm going to explain to you what a syllogism is.

OLD GENTLEMAN. Ah, yes, a syllogism.

JEAN. *(To* BERENGER.*)* I can't get over it! It's unthinkable!

>   *(*BERENGER *yawns.)*

LOGICIAN. *(Crossing to left of the* OLD GENTLEMAN.*)* A syllogism consists of a main proposition, a secondary one, and a conclusion.

OLD GENTLEMAN. What conclusion?

>   *(The* LOGICIAN *exits downstage left. The* OLD GENTLEMAN *follows him off.)*

**JEAN.** I just can't get over it!

**BERENGER.** Yes, I can see you can't. Well, it was a rhinoceros – all right, so it was a rhinoceros. It's miles away by now – miles away.

**JEAN.** But you must see it's fantastic! A rhinoceros loose in the town, and you don't bat an eyelid. It shouldn't be allowed.

> (**BERENGER** *yawns.*)

Put your hand in front of your mouth.

**BERENGER.** Yais – yais – it shouldn't be allowed. It's dangerous. I hadn't realized. But don't worry about it, it won't get us here.

**JEAN.** We ought to protest to the Town Council. What's the Council there for?

**BERENGER.** *(He yawns, then quickly puts his hand to his mouth.)* Oh, excuse me.

> *(He rises and moves left center; trying to wake up.)*

Perhaps the rhinoceros escaped from the zoo.

**JEAN.** You're daydreaming.

**BERENGER.** But I'm wide awake.

**JEAN.** Awake or asleep, it's the same thing.

**BERENGER.** But there is some difference.

**JEAN.** That's not the point.

**BERENGER.** But you just said being awake and being asleep were the same thing...

**JEAN.** You didn't understand. There's no difference between dreaming awake and dreaming asleep.

**BERENGER.** *(Wandering upstage left.)* I do dream. Life is a dream.

**JEAN.** You're certainly dreaming when you say the rhinoceros escaped from the zoo –

**BERENGER.** I only said – perhaps.

**JEAN.** – because there's been no zoo in our town since the animals were destroyed in the plague – ages ago.

**BERENGER.** *(With the same indifference.)* Then perhaps it came from a circus.

*(He goes into the pissoir.)*

**JEAN.** What circus are you talking about?

**BERENGER.** I don't know – some travelling circus.

**JEAN.** You know perfectly well that the Council banned all travelling performers from the district. There haven't been any since we were children.

**BERENGER.** *(He comes from the pissoir and moves downstage center, trying unsuccessfully to stop yawning.)* In that case, maybe it's been hiding ever since in the surrounding swamps.

**JEAN.** The surrounding swamps! The surrounding swamps! My poor friend, you live in a thick haze of alcohol.

**BERENGER.** *(Naïvely.)* That's very true.

*(He feels his stomach.)*

*(Morosely.)* It seems to mount from my stomach.

**JEAN.** It's clouding your brain. Where do you know of any surrounding swamps? Our district is known as "Little Castille," because the land is so arid.

**BERENGER.** *(Surfeited and pretty weary.)* How do I know, then? Perhaps it's been hiding under a stone. Or maybe it's been nesting on some withered branch.

**JEAN.** If you think you're being witty, you're very much mistaken. You're just being a bore with – with your stupid paradoxes. You're incapable of talking seriously.

**BERENGER.** *(Moving and sitting left of the table right center.)* Today, yes, only today – because of – because of...

*(He indicates his head with a vague gesture.)*

**JEAN.** Today's the same as any other day.

**BERENGER.** Oh, not quite as much.

**JEAN.** Your witticisms are not very inspired.

**BERENGER.** I wasn't trying to be...

**JEAN.** *(Interrupting.)* I can't bear people to try and make fun of me.

**BERENGER.** *(With his hand over his heart.)* But, my dear Jean, I'd never allow myself to...

**JEAN.** *(Interrupting.)* My dear Berenger, you are allowing yourself...

**BERENGER.** Oh, no, never. I'd never allow myself to.

**JEAN.** Yes, you would; you've just done so.

**BERENGER.** But how could you possibly think...?

**JEAN.** *(Interrupting.)* I think what is true.

**BERENGER.** But I assure you...

**JEAN.** *(Interrupting.)* That you were making fun of me.

**BERENGER.** You really can be obstinate, sometimes.

**JEAN.** And now you're calling me a mule, into the bargain. Even you must see how insulting you're being.

**BERENGER.** It would never have entered my mind.

**JEAN.** You have no mind.

**BERENGER.** All the more reason why it would never enter it.

**JEAN.** There are certain things which enter the minds of even people without them.

**BERENGER.** That's impossible.

**JEAN.** And why, pray, is it impossible?

**BERENGER.** Because it's impossible.

**JEAN.** Then kindly explain to me why it's impossible, as you seem to imagine you can explain everything.

**BERENGER.** I don't imagine anything of the kind.

**JEAN.** Then why do you act as if you do? And, I repeat, why are you being so insulting to me?

**BERENGER.** I'm not insulting you. Far from it. You know what tremendous respect I have for you.

**JEAN.** In that case, why do you contradict me, making out that it's not dangerous to let a rhinoceros go racing about in the middle of the town – particularly on a Sunday morning when the streets are full of children – and adults, too?

**BERENGER.** A lot of them are in church. They don't run any risk –

**JEAN.** *(Interrupting.)* If you will allow me to finish – and at market time, too.

**BERENGER.** *(After a pause.)* I never said it wasn't dangerous to let a rhinoceros go racing about the town. I simply said I'd personally never considered the danger. It had never crossed my mind.

**JEAN.** You never consider anything.

**BERENGER.** All right, I agree. A rhinoceros roaming about is not a good thing.

**JEAN.** It shouldn't be allowed.

**BERENGER.** I agree. It shouldn't be allowed. It's ridiculous. But it's no reason for you and me to quarrel.

> *(He rises and looks offstage left.)*

Why go on at me just because some wretched perissodactyl happens to pass by? A stupid quadruped not worth talking about. And ferocious into the bargain. And which has already disappeared – which doesn't exist any longer.

> *(He moves above the table right center and picks up his drink.)*

Let's talk about something else, Jean, please.

> *(He yawns.)*

There are plenty of other subjects for conversation.

> *(He raises his glass.)*

To you.

**JEAN.** *(Putting his cane over **BERENGER**'s arm.)* Put that glass back on the table. You're not to drink it.

> *(He takes a large drink from his own glass, then puts the glass half-empty on the table.)*

> *(**BERENGER** continues to hold his glass, without putting it down, and without daring to drink from it either. **DAISY**, a young blonde*

*typist, enters upstage left and goes into the shop where she is seen talking to the* **GROCER** *and his* **WIFE**.)

**BERENGER**. *(Timidly.)* There's no point in leaving it for the proprietor.

*(He raises his glass to his lips.)*

**JEAN**. Put it down, I tell you.

**BERENGER**. Very well.

(**DAISY**, *in the shop, laughs. Her laugh is recognized by* **BERENGER** *who turns abruptly and spills his drink over* **JEAN**'*s trousers.)*

Oh, there's Daisy.

*(He puts the glass on the table.)*

**JEAN**. *(Rising.)* Look out!

*(He crosses to center and wipes his trousers with his handkerchief.)*

How clumsy you are!

**BERENGER**. That's Daisy – I'm so sorry –

*(He hides right of the pissoir.)*

I don't want her to see me in this state.

**JEAN**. Your behaviour's unforgivable, absolutely unforgivable.

(**DAISY** *comes from the shop and exits downstage left. He looks after* **DAISY**.)

Why are you afraid of that young girl?

**BERENGER**. *(Running to right of* **JEAN**.) Oh, be quiet, please be quiet.

**JEAN**. She doesn't look an unpleasant person.

**BERENGER**. *(Kneeling and wiping* **JEAN**'*s trousers with his handkerchief.)* I must apologize once more for –

**JEAN**. You see what comes of drinking – you can no longer control your movements, you've no strength left in your hands, you're besotted and fagged out.

*(He moves a step or two left after a pause.)*

**JEAN**. You're digging your own grave, my friend, you're destroying yourself.

> *(There is a pause. **BERENGER** rises and wanders downstage right **JEAN** leans on the table left center.)*

**BERENGER**. I don't like the taste of alcohol much.

> *(He moves above the table right center.)*

And yet if I don't drink, I'm done for; it's as if I'm frightened, and so I drink not to be frightened any longer.

**JEAN**. Frightened of what?

**BERENGER**. *(Moving downstage left of the table right center.)* I don't know exactly. It's a sort of anguish difficult to describe. I feel out of place in life, among people, and so I take to drink. That calms me down and relaxes me so I can forget.

**JEAN**. You try to escape from yourself.

**BERENGER**. *(Sitting left of the table right center.)* I'm so tired. I've been tired for years. It's exhausting to drag the weight of my own body about.

**JEAN**. That's alcoholic neurasthenia, drinker's gloom.

**BERENGER**. I'm conscious of my body all the time, as if it were made of lead, or as if I were carrying another man around on my back. I can't seem to get used to myself. I don't even know if I *am* me. Then as soon as I take a drink, the lead slips away and I recognize myself, I become me again.

> *(The **OLD GENTLEMAN** and the **LOGICIAN** enter downstage left, deep in talk.)*

**JEAN**. That's being fanciful. Look at me, Berenger, I weigh more than you do. And yet I feel light, light as a feather.

> *(He airily raises his cane.)*

**LOGICIAN**. *(To the **OLD GENTLEMAN**.)* An example of syllogism –

*(***JEAN** *turns, bumps into the* **OLD GENTLEMAN** *which precipitates him into the arms of the* **LOGICIAN**.*)*

**LOGICIAN.** Oh!

**OLD GENTLEMAN.** *(To* **JEAN**.*)* Look out!

*(The* **OLD GENTLEMAN** *crosses canes with* **JEAN** *for a moment, then turns to the* **LOGICIAN**.*)*

I'm so sorry.

*(***BERENGER** *rises.)*

**JEAN.** *(To the* **OLD GENTLEMAN**.*)* I'm so sorry.

**LOGICIAN.** *(To the* **OLD GENTLEMAN**.*)* No harm done.

**OLD GENTLEMAN.** *(To* **JEAN**.*)* No harm done.

*(The* **OLD GENTLEMAN** *and the* **LOGICIAN** *move slowly counter-clockwise round the pissoir. Jean crosses to center.* **BERENGER** *resumes his seat left of the table right center.)*

**BERENGER.** *(To* **JEAN**.*)* You certainly are strong.

**JEAN.** Yes, I'm strong.

*(He crosses and stands upstage right of the table right center.)*

I'm strong for several reasons. In the first place I'm strong because I'm naturally strong –

*(He goes into a "Mr. Universe" pose.)*

and secondly I'm strong because I have moral strength.

*(He sits right of the table right center.)*

I'm also strong because I'm not riddled with alcohol. I don't wish to offend you, my dear Berenger, but I feel I must tell you that it's alcohol which weighs so heavy on you.

*(He takes out a nail file and files his nails.)*

*(The* **OLD GENTLEMAN** *and the* **LOGICIAN** *stop right of the pissoir. The* **LOGICIAN** *is right of the* **OLD GENTLEMAN**.*)*

**LOGICIAN.** *(To the* **OLD GENTLEMAN.***)* Here is an example of a syllogism. A cat has four paws. Isidore and Fricot both have four paws. Therefore Isidore and Fricot are cats.

**OLD GENTLEMAN.** My dog has got four paws.

**LOGICIAN.** Then it's a cat.

> *(The* **OLD GENTLEMAN** *and the* **LOGICIAN** *move downstage center.)*

**BERENGER.** *(To* **JEAN.***)* I've barely got the strength to go on living. Maybe I don't even want to.

> *(The* **OLD GENTLEMAN** *pauses downstage center, in deep reflection. The* **LOGICIAN** *moves downstage left of the pissoir.)*

**OLD GENTLEMAN.** *(After a pause; to the* **LOGICIAN.***)* So then logically speaking, my dog must be a cat?

**LOGICIAN.** *(Stopping for a moment.)* Logically, yes.

> *(He moves upstage left. The* **OLD GENTLEMAN** *scuttles to catch up with the* **LOGICIAN.***)*

But the contrary is also true.

> *(The* **OLD GENTLEMAN** *and the* **LOGICIAN** *pass above the pissor to right of it.)*

**BERENGER.** *(To* **JEAN.***)* Solitude seems to oppress me. And so does the company of other people.

**JEAN.** You contradict yourself. What oppresses you – solitude or the company of others? You consider yourself a thinker, yet you're devoid of logic.

**OLD GENTLEMAN.** *(To the* **LOGICIAN.***)* Logic is a very beautiful thing.

**LOGICIAN.** As long as it is not abused.

> *(The* **OLD GENTLEMAN** *and the* **LOGICIAN** *cross downstage left center.)*

**BERENGER.** *(To* **JEAN.***)* Life is an abnormal business.

**JEAN.** On the contrary. Nothing could be more natural, and the proof is that people go on living.

**BERENGER.** There are more dead people than living. And their numbers are increasing. The living are getting rarer.

**JEAN.** The dead don't exist, there's no getting away from that. *(He gives a huge laugh.)* Yet you're oppressed by them, too? How can you be oppressed by something that doesn't exist?

**BERENGER.** I sometimes wonder if I exist myself.

**JEAN.** You don't exist, my dear Berenger, because you don't think. Start thinking, then you will.

**LOGICIAN.** *(To the* **OLD GENTLEMAN.***)* Another syllogism. All cats die. Socrates is dead. Therefore Socrates is a cat.

**OLD GENTLEMAN.** And he's got four paws. That's true. I've got a cat named Socrates.

**LOGICIAN.** There you are, you see.

> *(The* **OLD GENTLEMAN** *and the* **LOGICIAN** *turn and pass above the pissoir to right of it.)*

**JEAN.** *(To* **BERENGER.***)* You're just fooling yourself, my dear chap. You say that life doesn't interest you. And yet there's somebody who does.

**BERENGER.** Who?

**JEAN.** Your little friend from the office who just went past. You're very fond of her.

> *(He chuckles loudly.)*

**OLD GENTLEMAN.** *(To the* **LOGICIAN.***)* So Socrates was a cat, was he?

> *(***BERENGER** *reacts to the* **OLD GENTLEMAN***'s line.)*

**LOGICIAN.** Logic has just revealed the fact to us.

> *(The* **OLD GENTLEMAN** *and the* **LOGICIAN** *cross downstage left center.)*

**JEAN.** *(To* **BERENGER.***)* You didn't want her to see you in your present state.

> *(***BERENGER** *makes a gesture.)*

**JEAN.** That proves you're not indifferent to everything. But how can you expect Daisy to be attracted to a drunkard?

**LOGICIAN.** *(To the* **OLD GENTLEMAN.***)* Let's get back to our cats.

**OLD GENTLEMAN.** I'm all ears.

**BERENGER.** *(To* **JEAN.***)* In any case, I think she's already got her eye on someone.

**JEAN.** Oh, who?

**BERENGER.** Dudard. An office colleague, qualified in law, with a big future in the firm – and in Daisy's affections. I can't hope to compete with him.

**LOGICIAN.** *(To the* **OLD GENTLEMAN.***)* The cat Isidore has four paws.

**OLD GENTLEMAN.** How do you know?

**LOGICIAN.** It's stated in the hypothesis.

**BERENGER.** *(To* **JEAN.***)* The chief thinks a lot of him. Whereas I've no future, I've no qualifications. I don't stand a chance.

**OLD GENTLEMAN.** *(To the* **LOGICIAN.***)* Ah! In the hypothesis.

**JEAN.** *(To* **BERENGER.***)* So you're giving up, just like that?

**BERENGER.** What else can I do?

**LOGICIAN.** *(To the* **OLD GENTLEMAN.***)* Fricot also has four paws. So how many paws have Fricot and Isidore?

**OLD GENTLEMAN.** Separately or together?

**JEAN.** *(To* **BERENGER.***)* Life is a struggle, it's cowardly not to put up a fight.

**LOGICIAN.** *(To the* **OLD GENTLEMAN.***)* Separately or together –

> *(The* **OLD GENTLEMAN** *moves up left center, thinking.)*

– it all depends.

**BERENGER.** *(To* **JEAN.***)* What can I do? I've nothing to put up a fight with.

**JEAN.** Then find yourself some weapons, my friend.

**OLD GENTLEMAN.** *(Moving to right of the* **LOGICIAN***; after painful reflection.)* Eight – eight paws.

**LOGICIAN.** Logic involves mental arithmetic, you see.

**OLD GENTLEMAN.** It certainly has many aspects.

**BERENGER.** *(To* **JEAN.***)* Where can I find the weapons?

**LOGICIAN.** *(To the* **OLD GENTLEMAN.***)* There are no limits to logic.

**JEAN.** *(To* **BERENGER.***)* Within yourself. Through your own will.

**BERENGER.** What weapons?

**LOGICIAN.** *(To the* **OLD GENTLEMAN.***)* I'm going to show you.

> *(The* **LOGICIAN** *and the* **OLD GENTLEMAN** *cross to right center.)*

**JEAN.** *(To* **BERENGER.***)* The weapons of patience and culture, the weapons of the mind.

> *(***BERENGER** *yawns.)*

Turn yourself into a keen and brilliant intellect. Get yourself up to the mark.

**BERENGER.** How do I get myself up to the mark?

**LOGICIAN.** *(To the* **OLD GENTLEMAN.***)* If I take two paws away from these cats – how many does each have left?

**OLD GENTLEMAN.** That's not so easy.

**BERENGER.** *(To* **JEAN.***)* That's not so easy.

**LOGICIAN.** *(To the* **OLD GENTLEMAN.***)* On the contrary, it's simple.

**OLD GENTLEMAN.** It may be simple for you, but not for me.

**BERENGER.** *(To* **JEAN.***)* It may be simple for you, but not for me.

> *(The* **LOGICIAN** *and the* **OLD GENTLEMAN** *cross to the table left center.)*

**LOGICIAN.** *(To the* **OLD GENTLEMAN.***)* Come on, exercise your mind. Concentrate.

**JEAN.** *(To* **BERENGER.***)* Come on, exercise your will. Concentrate.

**OLD GENTLEMAN.** *(Crossing to left of the table left center; to the* **LOGICIAN.***)* I don't see how.

**BERENGER.** *(To* **JEAN.***)* I really don't see how.

**LOGICIAN.** *(To the* **OLD GENTLEMAN.***)* You have to be told everything.

**JEAN.** *(To* **BERENGER.***)* You have to be told everything.

**LOGICIAN.** *(To the* **OLD GENTLEMAN.***)* Take a sheet of paper and calculate.

>    *(He sits right of the table left center.)*

If you take two paws from the two cats, how many paws are left to each cat?

**OLD GENTLEMAN.** *(Sitting left of the table left center.)* Just a moment.

>    *(He takes a piece of paper and a pencil from his pocket and calculates.)*

**JEAN.** *(To* **BERENGER.***)* This is what you must do: dress yourself properly, shave every day, put on a clean shirt.

**BERENGER.** The laundry's so expensive.

**JEAN.** Cut down on your drinking. This is the way to come out –

>    *(As he mentions the items of clothing he points self-contentedly to his own.)*

wear a hat, a tie like this, a well-cut coat, shoes well polished.

**OLD GENTLEMAN.** *(To the* **LOGICIAN.***)* There are several possible solutions.

**LOGICIAN.** Tell me.

**BERENGER.** *(To* **JEAN.***)* Then what do I do? Tell me.

**LOGICIAN.** *(To the* **OLD GENTLEMAN.***)* I'm listening.

**BERENGER.** *(To* **JEAN.***)* I'm listening.

**JEAN.** You're a timid creature, but not without talent.

**BERENGER.** I've got talent, me?

**JEAN.** So use it. Put yourself in the picture. Keep abreast of the cultural and literary events of the times.

**OLD GENTLEMAN.** *(To the* **LOGICIAN.***)* One possibility is: one cat could have four paws and the other two.

**BERENGER.** *(To* **JEAN.***)* I get so little spare time.

**LOGICIAN.** *(To the* **OLD GENTLEMAN.***)* You're not without talent. You just needed to exercise it.

**JEAN.** *(To* **BERENGER.***)* Take advantage of what free time you *do* have. Don't just let yourself drift.

**OLD GENTLEMAN.** *(To the* **LOGICIAN.***)* I've never had the time. I was an official, you know.

**LOGICIAN.** One can always find time to learn.

**JEAN.** *(To* **BERENGER.***)* One can always find time.

**BERENGER.** It's too late now.

**OLD GENTLEMAN.** *(To the* **LOGICIAN.***)* It's a bit late in the day for me.

**JEAN.** *(To* **BERENGER.***)* It's never too late.

**LOGICIAN.** *(To the* **OLD GENTLEMAN.***)* It's never too late.

**JEAN.** *(To* **BERENGER.***)* You work eight hours a day, like me and everybody else, but not on Sundays, nor in the evening, nor for three weeks in the summer. That's quite sufficient, with a little method.

**LOGICIAN.** *(To the* **OLD GENTLEMAN.***)* Well, what about the other solutions? Use a little method, a little method.

*(The* **OLD GENTLEMAN** *calculates.)*

**JEAN.** *(To* **BERENGER.***)* Look, instead of drinking and feeling sick, isn't it better to be fresh and eager, even at work? And you can spend your free time constructively.

**BERENGER.** How do you mean?

**JEAN.** By visiting museums, reading literary periodicals, going to lectures. That'll solve your troubles, it will develop your mind. In four weeks you'll be a cultured man.

**BERENGER.** You're right!

**OLD GENTLEMAN.** *(To the* **LOGICIAN.***)* There could be one cat with five paws –

**JEAN.** *(To* **BERENGER.***)* You see, you even think so yourself.

**OLD GENTLEMAN.** – and one cat with one paw. But would they still be cats, then?

LOGICIAN. Why not?

JEAN. *(To* BERENGER.*)* Instead of squandering all your spare money on drink, isn't it better to buy a ticket for an interesting play? Do you know anything about the *avant-garde* theatre there's so much talk about? Have you seen Ionesco's plays?

BERENGER. Unfortunately no. I've only heard people talk about them.

OLD GENTLEMAN. *(To the* LOGICIAN.*)* By taking two of the eight paws away from the two cats –

JEAN. *(To* BERENGER.*)* There's one playing now. Take advantage of it.

OLD GENTLEMAN. – we could have one cat with six paws –

BERENGER. *(To* JEAN.*)* It would be an excellent initiation into the artistic life of our times.

OLD GENTLEMAN. – we could have one cat with no paws at all.

BERENGER. *(To* JEAN.*)* You're right, perfectly right. I'm going to put myself into the picture, like you said.

LOGICIAN. *(To the* OLD GENTLEMAN.*)* In that case, one cat would be specially privileged.

BERENGER. *(To* JEAN.*)* I will, I promise you.

JEAN. You promise yourself, that's the main thing.

OLD GENTLEMAN. *(To the* LOGICIAN.*)* And one underprivileged cat deprived of all paws.

BERENGER. *(To* JEAN.*)* I make myself a solemn promise, I'll keep my word to myself.

LOGICIAN. *(To the* OLD GENTLEMAN.*)* That would be unjust, and therefore not logical.

BERENGER. *(To* JEAN.*)* Instead of drinking, I'll develop my mind. I feel better already. My head already feels clearer.

JEAN. You see!

OLD GENTLEMAN. *(To the* LOGICIAN.*)* Not logical?

**BERENGER.** *(To* **JEAN.***)* This afternoon I'll go to the museum. And I'll book two seats for the theatre this evening. Will you come with me?

**LOGICIAN.** *(To the* **OLD GENTLEMAN.***)* Because Logic means Justice.

**JEAN.** *(To* **BERENGER.***)* You must persevere. Keep up your good resolutions.

**OLD GENTLEMAN.** *(To the* **LOGICIAN.***)* I get it. Justice.

**BERENGER.** *(To* **JEAN.***)* I promise you, and I promise myself. Will you come to the museum with me this afternoon?

**JEAN.** I have to take a rest this afternoon: it's in my program for the day.

**OLD GENTLEMAN.** *(To the* **LOGICIAN.***)* Justice is one more aspect of logic.

**BERENGER.** *(To* **JEAN.***)* But you will come with me to theatre this evening?

**JEAN.** No, not this evening.

**LOGICIAN.** *(To the* **OLD GENTLEMAN.***)* Your mind is getting clearer.

**JEAN.** *(To* **BERENGER.***)* I sincerely hope you'll keep up your good resolutions. But this evening I have to meet some friends for a drink.

**BERENGER.** For a drink?

**OLD GENTLEMAN.** *(To the* **LOGICIAN.***)* What's more, a cat with no paws at all –

**JEAN.** *(To* **BERENGER.***)* I've promised to go. I always keep my word.

**OLD GENTLEMAN.** – wouldn't be able to run fast enough to catch mice.

**BERENGER.** *(To* **JEAN.***)* Ah, now it's you that's setting me a bad example. You're going out drinking.

**LOGICIAN.** *(To the* **OLD GENTLEMAN.***)* You're already making progress in logic.

*(Cue No. 03: Rhino charge.)*

*(The sound of rapid galloping is heard approaching off left, with trumpeting and the sound of rhinoceros hooves and pantings.)*

JEAN. *(To* BERENGER*; furiously.)* It's not a habit with me, you know. It's not the same as with you. With you – you're – it's not the same thing at all.

BERENGER. Why isn't it the same thing?

JEAN. *(Shouting over the noise.)* I'm no drunkard, not me.

LOGICIAN. *(Shouting to the* OLD GENTLEMAN*.)* Even with no paws a cat must catch mice. That's in its nature.

BERENGER. *(Shouting very loudly.)* I didn't mean you were a drunkard. But why would it make me one any more than you, in a case like that?

OLD GENTLEMAN. *(Shouting to the* LOGICIAN*.)* What's in the cat's nature?

JEAN. *(To* BERENGER*.)* Because there's moderation in all things. I'm a moderate person, not like you.

LOGICIAN. *(To the* OLD GENTLEMAN*; cupping his hands to his ears.)* What did you say?

*(Deafening sounds drown the words of the four characters.)*

BERENGER. *(To* JEAN*; cupping his hands to his ears.)* What about me – what? What did you say?

JEAN. *(Roaring.)* I said that –

OLD GENTLEMAN. *(Roaring.)* I said that –

JEAN. *(Suddenly aware of the noises which are now very near.)* Whatever's happening?

LOGICIAN. What is going on?

JEAN. *(He rises, knocks his chair over as he does so, and looks off left.)* Oh, a rhinoceros!

LOGICIAN. *(He rises, knocks over his chair and looks off left.)* Oh! A rhinoceros!

OLD GENTLEMAN. *(He rises, knocks over his chair and looks off left.)* Oh, a rhinoceros!

BERENGER. *(He remains seated but this time takes more notice.)* Rhinoceros! In the opposite direction!

*(The* **WAITRESS** *enters from the café carrying a tray of glasses and crosses to left of* **BERENGER**.*)*

**WAITRESS.** What is it?

*(She looks off left.)*

Oh, a rhinoceros!

*(She drops the tray, breaking the glasses.)*

*(The* **PROPRIETOR** *enters from the café.)*

**PROPRIETOR.** What's going on?

*(He picks up* **JEAN**'*s chair, then moves left, above the others.)*

**WAITRESS.** *(To the* **PROPRIETOR**.*)* A rhinoceros!

**LOGICIAN.** A rhinoceros, going full-tilt on the opposite pavement.

*(Sound loud.)*

*(The* **GROCER** *enters from his shop and looks off left.)*

**GROCER.** Oh, a rhinoceros!

**JEAN.** Oh, a rhinoceros!

*(The* **GROCER'S WIFE** *looks out of the upstairs window of the shop.)*

*(Cue No. 03: Sound fading.)*

**GROCER'S WIFE.** Oh, a rhinoceros!

**PROPRIETOR.** *(To the* **WAITRESS**.*)* It's no reason to break the glasses.

**JEAN.** It's rushing straight ahead, brushing up against the shop windows.

*(***DAISY** *runs on downstage left, stands below the table left center and looks off left.)*

**DAISY.** Oh, a rhinoceros!

**BERENGER.** *(Seeing* **DAISY**.*)* Oh – Daisy!

*(He rises and crosses down right to avoid being seen.)*

*(Cries of "oh" and "ah" and the sounds of people running are heard off left.)*

**WAITRESS.** Well, of all things!

**PROPRIETOR.** You'll be charged up for those.

**OLD GENTLEMAN, LOGICIAN, GROCER & GROCER'S WIFE.** Well, of all things!

*(Sound out.)*

**JEAN & BERENGER.** Well, of all things!

*(Cue A: A piteous mewing is heard off left.)*

**HOUSEWIFE.** *(Offstage left; crying piteously.)* Ah! All. Oh!

*(The noise dies rapidly away. The **HOUSEWIFE** runs on down left, without her basket, but holding the bloodstained corpse of her cat by the tail.)*

*(Wailing.)* It ran over my cat, it ran over my cat.

*(She cradles the cat in her arms and goes up center, sobbing.)*

*(The **GROCER**, the **OLD GENTLEMAN**, **DAISY**, and the **LOGICIAN** follow the **HOUSEWIFE** and crowd round her.)*

**ALL.** What a tragedy, poor little thing.

**OLD GENTLEMAN.** Poor little thing!

**DAISY & WAITRESS.** Poor little thing!

**GROCER'S WIFE, OLD GENTLEMAN & LOGICIAN.** Poor little thing!

*(The **PROPRIETOR** stands the chair left upright and turns to the **WAITRESS**.)*

**PROPRIETOR.** *(Indicating the broken glasses.)* Don't just stand there! Clear up the mess!

*(**JEAN** and **BERENGER** join the others round the **HOUSEWIFE**, who continues to lament, her dead cat in her arms.)*

**WAITRESS.** *(Kneeling and collecting the tray and broken glass.)* Oh, poor little thing!

**OLD GENTLEMAN.** *(To the* **GROCER.***)* Well, what do you think of that?

**BERENGER.** *(To the* **HOUSEWIFE.***)* You mustn't cry like that, it's too heartbreaking.

**DAISY.** *(Moving to left of* **BERENGER.***)* Were you there, Mr. Berenger? Did you see it?

**BERENGER.** Good morning, Miss Daisy. You must excuse me, I haven't had a chance to shave.

> *(He backs away right.)*

> *(The* **PROPRIETOR** *stands the chair center upright, then stands right center in front of the café.)*

**PROPRIETOR.** Poor little thing!

**WAITRESS.** *(Rising with the tray and debris and crossing to right of the* **PROPRIETOR.***)* Poor little thing!

> *(These remarks must obviously be made very rapidly, almost simultaneously. The* **HOUSEWIFE** *moves down left center. The group round her follow, with the exception of* **DAISY** *who moves to right of the pissoir.)*

**GROCER'S WIFE.** *(At the window.)* That's going too far!

**JEAN.** That's going too far!

**HOUSEWIFE.** *(Lamenting.)* My poor little pussy, my poor little cat!

> *(The* **OLD GENTLEMAN** *stands right of the* **HOUSEWIFE,** *the* **LOGICIAN** *is left of her,* **JEAN** *and the* **GROCER** *are behind her.)*

**OLD GENTLEMAN.** *(To the* **HOUSEWIFE.***)* What can you do, dear lady – cats are only mortal.

**LOGICIAN.** What do you expect, madam? All cats are mortal. One must accept that.

**HOUSEWIFE.** *(Lamenting.)* My little cat, my poor little cat.

**PROPRIETOR.** *(To the* **WAITRESS***; indicating the broken glass.)* Throw that in the dustbin.

*(The others all look at the* **PROPRIETOR***.)*

*(To the* **WAITRESS***.)* You owe me a thousand francs.

**WAITRESS.** All you think of is money.

*(The* **WAITRESS** *exits to the café.)*

**GROCER'S WIFE.** *(Calling to the* **HOUSEWIFE***.)* Don't upset yourself.

**OLD GENTLEMAN.** *(To the* **HOUSEWIFE***.)* Don't upset yourself, dear lady.

**GROCER'S WIFE.** It's very upsetting, a thing like that.

**HOUSEWIFE.** *(Moving downstage left center; sobbing.)* My little cat, my little cat.

**DAISY.** Yes, it's very upsetting, a thing like that.

**OLD GENTLEMAN.** *(Ushering the* **HOUSEWIFE** *to the table left center.)* Sit down here, dear lady.

**JEAN.** *(To the* **OLD GENTLEMAN***.)* Well, what do you think of that?

**GROCER** *(To the* **LOGICIAN***.)* Well, what do you think of that?

**GROCER'S WIFE.** *(Calling to* **DAISY***.)* Well, what do you think of that?

*(The* **WAITRESS** *enters from the café.)*

**PROPRIETOR** *(To the* **WAITRESS***.)* A glass of water for the lady.

**OLD GENTLEMAN.** *(To the* **HOUSEWIFE***.)* Sit down, dear lady.

*(The* **HOUSEWIFE** *sits on the chair left of the table left center.* **DAISY** *moves and stands above the table left center. The* **OLD GENTLEMAN** *stands left of* **DAISY***. The* **LOGICIAN** *is left center. The* **GROCER** *is left. The* **GROCER***'s* **WIFE** *is still at the window.* **BERENGER** *is downstage right.* **JEAN** *moves downstage left. The* **PROPRIETOR** *is right center. The* **WAITRESS** *is right of the* **PROPRIETOR***.)*

**JEAN.** Poor woman!

**GROCER'S WIFE.** Poor cat!

**BERENGER.** *(Moving downstage right of the table right center.)* Better give her a brandy.

**PROPRIETOR.** *(To the* **WAITRESS.***)* A brandy.

> *(He points to* **BERENGER.***)*

This gentleman is paying.

**WAITRESS.** One brandy, right away.

> *(The* **WAITRESS** *exits to the café.)*

**HOUSEWIFE.** *(Sobbing.)* I don't want any, I don't want any!

**GROCER.** *(Moving in a little.)* It went past my shop a little while ago.

**JEAN.** *(Moving above the table left center; to the* **GROCER.***)* It wasn't the same one.

**GROCER.** But I could have –

**GROCER'S WIFE.** Yes, it was, it was the same one.

**DAISY.** Did it go past twice, then?

**PROPRIETOR.** I think it was the same one.

**JEAN.** No, it was not the same rhinoceros. The one that went by first had two horns on its nose, it was an Asiatic rhinoceros; this only had one, it was an African rhinoceros.

> *(He moves downstage left.)*

> *(The* **WAITRESS** *enters from the café and moves to the table left center. She carries a tray with a brandy on it.)*

**OLD GENTLEMAN.** *(To the* **HOUSEWIFE.***)* Here's a drop of brandy to pull you together.

**HOUSEWIFE.** *(In tears.)* No-o-o.

**BERENGER.** *(He moves right of the* **PROPRIETOR.** *To* **JEAN***; suddenly unnerved.)* You're talking nonsense! How could you possibly tell about the horns? The animal flashed past at such a speed, we hardly even saw it.

**DAISY.** *(To the* **HOUSEWIFE.***)* Go on, it will do you good.

**OLD GENTLEMAN.** *(To* **JEAN.***)* Very true. It did go fast.

(**JEAN** *moves above the table left center and stands between the* **PROPRIETOR** *and the* **LOGICIAN**.)

**PROPRIETOR.** *(To the* **HOUSEWIFE**.*)* Just have a taste – it's good.

**BERENGER.** *(To* **JEAN**.*)* You had no time to count its horns.

**GROCER'S WIFE.** *(Calling to the* **WAITRESS**.*)* Make her drink it.

**BERENGER.** *(To* **JEAN**.*)* What's more, it was travelling in a cloud of dust.

**DAISY.** *(To the* **HOUSEWIFE**.*)* Drink it up.

**OLD GENTLEMAN.** Just a sip, dear little lady. Be brave.

(*The* **WAITRESS** *forces the* **HOUSEWIFE** *to drink by putting the glass to her lips. The* **HOUSEWIFE** *feigns refusal, but drinks all the same.*)

**WAITRESS.** There, you see!

**GROCER'S WIFE & DAISY.** There, you see!

**JEAN.** *(To* **BERENGER**.*)* I don't have to grope my way through a fog. I can calculate quickly – my mind is clear.

**OLD GENTLEMAN.** *(To the* **HOUSEWIFE**.*)* Better now?

**BERENGER.** *(To* **JEAN**.*)* But it had its head thrust down.

**PROPRIETOR.** *(To the* **HOUSEWIFE**.*)* Now, wasn't that good?

**JEAN.** *(To* **BERENGER**.*)* Precisely. One could see all the better.

**HOUSEWIFE.** My little cat!

**BERENGER.** *(Moving above the table right center; irritated.)* Utter nonsense!

**GROCER'S WIFE.** *(To the* **HOUSEWIFE**.*)* I've got another cat you can have.

**JEAN.** *(To* **BERENGER**.*)* What, me? You dare to accuse me of talking nonsense?

**HOUSEWIFE.** *(To the* **GROCER'S WIFE**.*)* I'll never have another.

(*She weeps and cradles the cat.*)

**BERENGER.** *(To* **JEAN**.*)* Yes, absolute blithering nonsense!

**PROPRIETOR.** *(To the* **HOUSEWIFE.***)* You have to accept these things.

**JEAN.** *(Crossing to left of* **BERENGER.***)* I've never talked nonsense in my life.

**OLD GENTLEMAN.** *(To the* **HOUSEWIFE.***)* Try and be philosophic about it.

**BERENGER.** *(To* **JEAN.***)* You're just a pretentious show-off – *(He raises his voice.)* a pedant!

**PROPRIETOR.** Now, gentlemen!

**BERENGER.** *(He moves downstage right.)* And what's more, a pedant who's not cetrain of his facts because in the first place it's the Asiatic rhinoceros with only one horn on its nose, and it's the African with two.

> *(The others turn away from the* **HOUSEWIFE** *and watch* **JEAN** *and* **BERENGER** *who argue at the tops of their voices.)*

**JEAN.** You're wrong, it's the other way about.

**HOUSEWIFE.** He was so sweet.

**BERENGER.** *(Swinging round to face* **JEAN.***)* Do you want to bet?

**WAITRESS.** *(Moving to left of* **JEAN.***)* They're going to make a bet.

**DAISY.** *(Running to left of* **BERENGER.***)* Don't excite yourself, Mr. Berenger.

**JEAN.** I'm not betting with you. If anybody's got two horns – it's you. You Asiatic Mongol.

**WAITRESS.** Oh!

**GROCER'S WIFE.** *(To the* **GROCER.***)* They're going to have a fight.

**GROCER.** Nonsense, it's just a bet.

**PROPRIETOR.** *(Moving between* **DAISY** *and* **JEAN.***)* We don't want any scenes here.

**BERENGER.** *(To* **JEAN.***)* I've got no horns. And I never will have.

**OLD GENTLEMAN.** *(Moving downstage left of the* **GROCER.***)* Now look. What kind has one horn? *(To the* **GROCER.***)* You're a tradesman, you should know.

**GROCER'S WIFE.** Yes, you should know.

**JEAN.** *(To* **BERENGER.***)* Oh, yes, you have.

**GROCER.** *(To the* **OLD GENTLEMAN.***)* Tradesmen can't be expected to know everything.

> *(The* **OLD GENTLEMAN** *crosses above the others to right center.)*

**BERENGER.** *(To* **JEAN.***)* I'm not Asiatic, either. And in any case, Asiatics are people the same as everyone else.

**WAITRESS.** Yes, Asiatics are people the same as we are.

**OLD GENTLEMAN.** *(To the* **PROPRIETOR.***)* That's true!

**PROPRIETOR.** *(To the* **WAITRESS.***)* Nobody's asking for your opinion.

**DAISY.** *(To the* **PROPRIETOR.***)* She's right. They're people the same as we are.

**HOUSEWIFE.** *(Lamenting.)* He was so gentle, just like one of us.

**JEAN.** *(Beside himself.)* They're yellow!

> *(The* **LOGICIAN** *follows the controversy attentively, without taking part.)*

Goodbye, gentlemen. *(To* **BERENGER.***)* You, I will not deign to include.

> *(He picks up his gloves and crosses to left center.)*

**HOUSEWIFE.** He was devoted to us.

> *(She sobs.)*

**DAISY.** Now listen a moment, Mr. Berenger, and you, too, Mr. Jean –

**OLD GENTLEMAN.** I once had some friends who were Asiatics. But perhaps they weren't real ones.

**PROPRIETOR.** I've known some real ones.

**WAITRESS.** *(To the* **OLD GENTLEMAN.***)* I had an Asiatic friend once.

**HOUSEWIFE.** *(Still sobbing.)* I had him when he was a little kitten.

**JEAN.** *(Moving downstage left and turning to face* **BERENGER***; still quite beside himself.)* They're yellow, I tell you, bright yellow.

**BERENGER.** *(Moving downstage center and facing* **JEAN.***)* Whatever they are, you're bright red.

**GROCER'S WIFE & WAITRESS.** Oh!

**PROPRIETOR.** This is getting serious.

> *(He picks up the glasses from the table right center.)*

**HOUSEWIFE.** He was so clean. He always used his tray.

**JEAN.** *(To* **BERENGER.***)* If that's how you feel, it's the last time you'll see me. I'm not wasting my time with a fool like you.

> *(***JEAN** *exits fast and furiously left.)*

**HOUSEWIFE.** He always made himself understood.

**OLD GENTLEMAN.** *(To the* **GROCER.***)* There are white Asiatics as well, and black and blue, and even some like us.

**JEAN.** *(He enters left center and crosses to left center. To* **BERENGER.***)* You drunkard!

> *(The others look at* **JEAN** *in consternation.)*

**ALL.** Ooh!

> *(***JEAN** *exits left.)*

**BERENGER.** *(Crossing to left.)* I'm not going to stand for that!

**ALL.** *(Looking off left.)* Oh!

**HOUSEWIFE.** He could almost talk – in fact he did.

**DAISY.** *(To* **BERENGER.***)* You shouldn't have made him angry.

**BERENGER.** *(Moving downstage left and turning to* **DAISY.***)* It wasn't my fault.

**PROPRIETOR.** *(To the* **WAITRESS.***)* Go and get a little coffin for the poor thing.

**OLD GENTLEMAN.** *(To* **BERENGER.***)* I think you're right. It's the Asiatic rhinoceros with two horns and the African with one.

**GROCER.** But he was saying the opposite.

**DAISY.** *(To* **BERENGER.***)* You were both wrong.

**OLD GENTLEMAN.** *(To* **BERENGER.***)* Even so, you were right.

> *(He moves away upstage right.)*

**WAITRESS.** *(Moving to left of the* **HOUSEWIFE** *and taking her arm.)* Come with me, we're going to put him in a little box.

**HOUSEWIFE.** *(Sobbing desperately.)* No, never!

**GROCER.** If you don't mind my saying so, I think Mr. Jean was right.

**DAISY.** *(She crosses to the* **HOUSEWIFE** *and takes her right arm.)* Now you must be reasonable.

> *(***DAISY** *and the* **WAITRESS** *raise the* **HOUSEWIFE** *and lead her toward the café.)*

**OLD GENTLEMAN.** *(To* **DAISY.***)* Would you like me to come with you?

**DAISY.** No, don't you bother.

> *(***DAISY** *and the* **WAITRESS** *lead the* **HOUSEWIFE** *off into the café. The* **OLD GENTLEMAN** *and the* **PROPRIETOR** *move and stand at the entrance.)*

**GROCER.** *(Moving downstage center.)* The Asiatic rhinoceros has one horn and the African rhinoceros has two. And *vice versa.*

**GROCER'S WIFE.** Oh, you always have to be different from everybody else.

> *(The* **GROCER** *moves upstage left center.)*

**BERENGER.** *(Aside.)* Daisy was right, I should never have contradicted him.

**PROPRIETOR.** *(To the* **GROCER'S WIFE.***)* Your husband's right, the Asiatic rhinoceros has one horn and the African one must have *two,* and *vice versa.*

**BERENGER.** *(Aside.)* He can't stand being contradicted. The slightest disagreement makes him fume.

> *(The* **LOGICIAN** *crosses upstage right deep in thought.)*

**OLD GENTLEMAN.** *(Moving to left of the* **PROPRIETOR** *and facing him.)* You're mistaken, my friend.

**PROPRIETOR.** I'm very sorry, I'm sure.

**BERENGER.** *(Aside.)* His temper's his only fault.

**GROCER'S WIFE.** *(Calling to the group right.)* Maybe they're both the same.

**BERENGER.** *(Aside.)* Deep down, he's got a heart of gold; he's done me many a good turn.

**PROPRIETOR.** *(To* **GROCER'S WIFE.***)* If the one has two horns, then the other must have one.

**OLD GENTLEMAN.** Perhaps it's the other with two and the one with one.

**BERENGER.** *(Aside.)* I'm sorry I wasn't more accommodating. But why is he so obstinate? I didn't want to exasperate him.

> *(He moves to right of the table left center.)*

*(To the others.)* He's always making fantastic statements. Always trying to dazzle people with his knowledge. He never will admit he's wrong.

**OLD GENTLEMAN.** *(Moving menacingly towards* **BERENGER.***)* Have you any proof?

**BERENGER.** *(Retreating to left center.)* Proof of what?

**OLD GENTLEMAN.** Of the statement you made just now which started the unfortunate row with your friend.

**GROCER.** *(To* **BERENGER.***)* Yes, have you any proof?

**OLD GENTLEMAN.** *(To* **BERENGER.***)* How do you know that one of the two rhinoceros has one horn and the other two?

*(He waves his cane at* **BERENGER**.*)*

**OLD GENTLEMAN**. And which is which?

**GROCER'S WIFE**. He doesn't know any more than we do.

**BERENGER**. *(Recovering and moving above the table left center.)* In the first place we don't know that there were two. I myself believe there was only one.

**PROPRIETOR**. Well, let's say there were two. Does the single-horned one come from Asia?

**OLD GENTLEMAN**. *(Crossing to left of the* **PROPRIETOR**.*)* No. It's the one from Africa with two, I think.

**PROPRIETOR**. Which is two-horned?

**GROCER**. It's not the one from Africa.

**GROCER'S WIFE**. It's not easy to agree on this.

**OLD GENTLEMAN**. But the problem must be cleared up.

**LOGICIAN**. *(Emerging from his isolation.)* Excuse me, gentlemen, for interrupting, but that is not the question. Allow me to introduce myself...

**HOUSEWIFE**. *(Tearfully.)* He's a logician.

**PROPRIETOR**. Oh, a logician, is he?

**OLD GENTLEMAN**. *(To* **BERENGER**; *introducing.)* My friend – the Logician.

**BERENGER**. Very happy to meet you.

**LOGICIAN** *(He takes a card from his pocket and moves to right of the table right center.)* Professional Logician.

*(He shows the card to* **BERENGER**.*)*

My card.

**BERENGER**. It's a great honor.

**GROCER**. A great honor for all of us.

**PROPRIETOR**. Would you mind telling us then, sir, if the African rhinoceros is single-horned?

**OLD GENTLEMAN**. Or bicorned?

**GROCER'S WIFE**. And is the Asiatic rhinoceros bicorned?

**GROCER**. Or unicorned?

**LOGICIAN**. Exactly, that is not the question.

*(He sits right of the table left center.* **BERENGER** *sits left of the table left center.)*

**LOGICIAN.** Let me make myself clear.

**GROCER.** *(Crossing and standing behind* **BERENGER**'s *chair.)* But it's still what we want to find out.

**LOGICIAN.** Kindly allow me to speak, gentlemen.

**OLD GENTLEMAN.** *(Moving behind the* **LOGICIAN**'s *chair.)* Let him speak.

**GROCER'S WIFE.** *(To the* **GROCER**.*)* Give him a chance to speak.

**PROPRIETOR.** *(Moving right center.)* We're listening, sir.

*(He sits right of the table right center.)*

**LOGICIAN.** *(To* **BERENGER**.*)* I'm addressing you in particular. And all the others present as well.

**GROCER.** Us as well.

**LOGICIAN.** You see, you have got away from the problem which instigated the debate. In the first place you were deliberating whether or not the rhinoceros which passed by just now was the same one that passed by earlier, or whether it was another. That is the question to decide.

**BERENGER.** Yes, but how?

**LOGICIAN.** Thus. You may have seen on two occasions a single rhinoceros bearing a single horn –

**GROCER.** *(Repeating the words as if to understand better.)* "...on two occasions a single rhinoceros..."

**PROPRIETOR.** "...bearing a single horn..."

**LOGICIAN.** – or you may have seen on two occasions a single rhinoceros with two horns.

**OLD GENTLEMAN.** A single rhinoceros with two horns on two occasions.

**LOGICIAN.** Exactly. Or again, you may have seen one rhinoceros with one horn, and then another also with a single horn.

**GROCER'S WIFE.** Ha, ha!

**LOGICIAN.** Or again, an initial rhinoceros with two horns, followed by a second with two horns.

**PROPRIETOR.** That's true.

**LOGICIAN.** Now, if you had seen –

**GROCER.** If we'd seen –

**OLD GENTLEMAN.** Yes, if we'd seen –

**LOGICIAN.** If on the first occasion you had seen a rhinoceros with two horns –

**PROPRIETOR.** With two horns –

**LOGICIAN.** – and on the second occasion, a rhinoceros with one horn –

**GROCER.** With one horn –

**LOGICIAN.** – that wouldn't be conclusive, either.

**OLD GENTLEMAN.** Even that wouldn't be conclusive.

**PROPRIETOR.** *(Rising and moving center.)* Why not?

**GROCER'S WIFE.** Oh, I don't get it at all.

**GROCER.** Shoo! Shoo!

> *(The* **GROCER'S WIFE** *shrugs her shoulders and withdraws from the window.)*

**LOGICIAN.** For it is possible that since its first appearance, the rhinoceros may have lost one of its horns, and that the first and second transit were still made by a single beast.

**BERENGER.** I see. But –

**OLD GENTLEMAN.** *(Interrupting.)* Don't interrupt!

**LOGICIAN.** It may also be that two rhinoceroses both with two horns may each have lost a horn.

**OLD GENTLEMAN.** That is possible.

**PROPRIETOR.** *(Sitting left of the table right center.)* Yes, that's possible.

**GROCER.** Why not?

**BERENGER.** Yes, but in any case –

**OLD GENTLEMAN.** Don't interrupt!

**LOGICIAN**. If you could prove that on the first occasion you saw a rhinoceros with one horn, either Asiatic or African –

**OLD GENTLEMAN**. Asiatic or African –

**LOGICIAN**. – and on the second occasion a rhinoceros with two horns –

**GROCER**. One with two –

**LOGICIAN**. – no matter whether African or Asiatic –

**OLD GENTLEMAN**. African or Asiatic...

**LOGICIAN**. – we could then conclude that we were dealing with two different rhinoceroses, for it is hardly likely that a second horn could grow sufficiently in a space of a few minutes to be visible on the nose of a rhinoceros.

**OLD GENTLEMAN**. It's hardly likely.

**LOGICIAN**. *(Enchanted with his discourse.)* That would imply one rhinoceros either Asiatic or African –

**OLD GENTLEMAN**. Asiatic or African –

**LOGICIAN**. – and one rhinoceros either African or Asiatic.

**PROPRIETOR**. African or Asiatic.

**GROCER**. Er – yais.

**LOGICIAN**. For good logic cannot entertain the possibility that the same creature be born in two places at the same time.

**OLD GENTLEMAN**. Or even successively.

**LOGICIAN**. Which was to be proved.

**BERENGER**. That seems clear enough, but it doesn't answer the question.

**LOGICIAN**. *(Rising; to* **BERENGER**, *with a knowledgeable smile.)* Obviously, my dear sir, but now the problem is correctly posed.

　　　*(He crosses downstage left.)*

**OLD GENTLEMAN**. It's quite logical. Quite logical.

**LOGICIAN**. *(Raising his hat.)* Goodbye, gentlemen.

　　　*(The* **LOGICIAN** *exits downstage left.)*

**OLD GENTLEMAN**. *(Crossing downstage left.)* Goodbye, gentlemen.

> *(The* **OLD GENTLEMAN** *exits down left.)*

**GROCER**. Well, it may be logical –

> *(The* **HOUSEWIFE**, *in deep mourning, enters from the café, carrying a box. She is followed by* **DAISY** *and the* **WAITRESS**, *as if for a funeral.* **BERENGER** *and the* **PROPRIETOR** *rise. The cortège crosses below the others toward the exit downstage left.)*

– it may be logical, but are we going to stand for our cats being run down under our very eyes by one-horned rhinoceroses *or* two, whether they're Asiatic *or* African?

> *(The* **HOUSEWIFE**, **DAISY**, *and the* **WAITRESS** *exit downstage left.)*

**PROPRIETOR**. He's absolutely right. We're not standing for our cats being run down by rhinoceroses or anything else.

> *(He collects the glasses and ashtray from the table right center, then crosses and clears the table left center.)*

**GROCER**. We're not going to stand for it.

> *(The* **GROCER'S WIFE** *appears at the shop door left.)*

**GROCER'S WIFE**. *(To the* **GROCER**.*)* Are you coming in? The customers will be here any minute.

> *(The* **GROCER'S WIFE** *withdraws.)*

**GROCER**. *(Crossing to the shop door.)* No, we're not standing for it.

> *(The* **GROCER** *exits to the shop.)*

**BERENGER**. I should never have quarrelled with Jean. *(To the* **PROPRIETOR**.*)* Get me a brandy. A double.

**PROPRIETOR**. Coming up.

*(The* **PROPRIETOR** *crosses and exits to the café, taking the dirty glasses and ashtrays with him.* **BERENGER,** *now alone, sits right of the table left center.)*

**BERENGER.** I never should have quarrelled with Jean. I shouldn't have got into such a rage.

*(The* **PROPRIETOR** *enters from the café with a large brandy. He crosses, gives the drink to* **BERENGER,** *then crosses and exits to the café.)*

I feel too upset to go to the museum. I'll cultivate my mind some other time.

*(***BERENGER** *drinks, put the glass on the table and exits upstage right. The lights dim to blackout, as:)*

*(Curtain.)*

## Scene Two

*(SCENE: The office of a firm of law publications. The following morning. The office is on an upper floor and is entered by a staircase which emerges through a trap, center. The trap is surrounded on three sides by a light balustrade or rail. Double doors left lead to* **MR. PAPILLON**'s *office. French windows upstage center, with exterior shutters, overlook the street. There are shelves in a shallow alcove right.* **DAISY**'s *typing table is left, with a typewriter on it. The chair is left of the table. There is a small table below the staircase center, with a chair above it. A larger table is right, with three stools, one each above, left and right of it. Wastepaper baskets stand below the table right, and above the table left. A hat stand is above the double doors left, and there is a filing cabinet right of the French windows. At night, the office is lit by two table lamps on the table right and wall-brackets above and below the double doors left.*

*(Cue No. 04: Clock strikes distantly – then typing.)*

*(In the Bristol production there was no interscene curtain and the scene was changed in view of the audience. When the scene was ready, the characters entered up the trap center, carrying stools, and the dialogue commenced while they were sorting out various properties.)*

*(AT RISE: It is three minutes past nine.* **BOTARD, DAISY, DUDARD,** *and* **MR. PAPILLON** *enter up the stairs.* **BOTARD,** *a brisk sixty-year-old, is a former school teacher. He is short,*

*has a proud air and a little white moustache. He wears a Basque beret, and wears a long grey blouse during working hours, with spectacles on a longish nose, a pencil behind his ear and protective sleeves. He knows everything, understands everything, judges everything. When he comes up the stairs he carries a stool.* **DAISY** *carries her handbag, a handful of papers, her notebook, pencils and a pencil sharpener.* **DUDARD** *is aged thirty-five. He is quite tall; a young employee with a future. He wears a grey suit, spectacles, and black lustrine sleeves to protect his coat. If the Department Head became the Assistant Director, he would take his place.* **BOTARD** *does not like him. He carries a stool and a newspaper.* **MR. PAPILLON,** *the Head of the Department, is about forty, very correctly dressed in a dark blue suit, with a rosette of the Legion of Honour, a starched collar, and a black tie. He has a large brown moustache. He carries a stool. During the first few moments the stools are set at the table right* **BOTARD** *removes his jacket, hangs it on the hat stand, takes down his overall and puts it on.* **PAPILLON** *goes to the cabinet upstage right and takes out some galley proofs and other documents.* **DAISY** *removes the typewriter cover and puts it on the hat stand.* **BOTARD,** **DUDARD,** *and* **DAISY** *sign the time sheet on the table center.)*

**BOTARD.** It's all a lot of made-up nonsense.

**DAISY.** But I saw it, I saw the rhinoceros.

**DUDARD.** It's in the paper, in black and white, you can't deny that.

**BOTARD.** *(With an air of greatest scorn.)* Pfff!

*(He moves above the table right.)*

**DUDARD**. It's all here; it's down here in the dead cats column. (*To* **PAPILLON**.) Read it for yourself, Chief.

> (*He holds out his newspaper.*)

> (**PAPILLON** *puts the proofs on the table right, moves to* **DUDARD** *and takes the newspaper from him.* **DUDARD** *goes upstage center.*)

**PAPILLON**. (*Reading.*) "Yesterday, just before lunch time, in the church square of our town, a cat was trampled to death by a pachyderm."

**DAISY**. (*Taking a compact from her handbag.*) It wasn't exactly in the church square.

**PAPILLON**. That's all it says.

> (*He puts the newspaper on the table right, hands some documents to* **DUDARD** *and the remainder to* **DAISY**.)

No other details.

> (*He goes to the table center, signs the time sheet, then moves left center.*)

**BOTARD**. Pfff.

> (*He crosses to the shelves right and collects his protective sleeves.*)

**DUDARD**. Well, that's clear enough.

**BOTARD** (*Putting on his sleeves.*) I never believe journalists. They're all liars. I don't need them to tell me what to think; I believe what I see with my own eyes. Speaking as a former teacher, I like things to be precise, scientifically valid; I've got a methodical mind.

> (**DAISY** *sits at her table left.*)

**DUDARD**. What's a methodical mind got to do with it?

**DAISY**. (*Powdering her nose.*) I think it's stated very precisely, Mr. Botard.

**BOTARD**. (*Picking up the newspaper.*) You call that precise? And what, pray, does it mean by "pachyderm"? What does the editor of a dead cats column understand by

a pachyderm? He doesn't say. And what does he mean
by a cat?

**DUDARD.** Everybody knows what a cat is.

**BOTARD.** Does it concern a male cat or a female? What
breed is it? And what color? The color bar is something
I feel strongly about. I hate it.

**PAPILLON.** What has the color bar to do with it, Mr. Botard?
It's quite beside the point.

**BOTARD.** Please forgive me, Mr. Papillon, but you can't deny
that the color problem is one of the great stumbling
blocks of our time.

**DUDARD.** *(Moving above the table right.)* I know that, we all
know that, but it has nothing to do with –

**BOTARD.** It's not an issue to be dismissed lightly,
Mr. Dudard. The course of history has shown that
racial prejudice –

**DUDARD.** *(Thumping the table.)* I tell you it doesn't enter
into it.

> *(***DAISY*** *puts her compact in her handbag and*
> *rises.)*

**BOTARD.** I'm not so sure.

**PAPILLON.** The color bar is not the issue at stake.

**BOTARD.** One should never miss an occasion to denounce
it.

**DAISY.** *(With an impatient gesture.)* But we told you that
none of us is in favour of the color bar. You're obscuring
the issue; it's simply a question of a cat being run over
by a pachyderm – in this case, a rhinoceros.

**BOTARD.** I'm a Northerner myself. Southerners have got
too much imagination. Perhaps it was merely a flea
run over by a mouse. People make mountains out of
molehills.

> *(He sits right of the tables right.)*

**PAPILLON.** *(Crossing to left of* **DUDARD**.) Let us try and get
things clear. *(To* **DUDARD**.) Did you yourself, with your

own eyes, see a rhinoceros strolling through the streets
of the town?

**DAISY.** It didn't stroll, it ran.

**DUDARD.** No, I didn't see it personally. But a lot of very
reliable people –

**BOTARD.** *(Interrupting.)* It's obvious they were just making
it up.

> *(He sharpens his pencil.)*

You put too much trust in these journalists; they don't
care what they invent to sell their wretched newspapers
and please the bosses they serve. And you mean to tell
me they've taken you in – you, a qualified man of law!
Forgive me for laughing. Ha, ha, ha!

**DAISY.** But I saw it, I saw the rhinoceros. I'd take my oath
on it.

**BOTARD.** Get away with you! And I thought you were a
sensible girl.

**DAISY.** Mr. Botard, I can see straight. And I wasn't the only
one; there were plenty of other people watching.

**BOTARD.** Pfff! They were probably watching something
else. A few idlers with nothing to do, work-shy loafers.

**DUDARD.** It happened yesterday – Sunday.

**BOTARD.** I work on Sundays as well. I've no time for
priests who do their utmost to get you to church, just
to prevent you from working, and earning your daily
bread by the sweat of your brow.

**PAPILLON.** *(Facing* **BOTARD** *across the table right;
indignantly.)* Oh!

**BOTARD.** I'm sorry, I didn't mean to offend you. The fact
that I despise religion doesn't mean I don't esteem it
highly. *(To* **DAISY.***)* In any case, do you know what a
rhinoceros looks like?

**DAISY.** It's a very big – ugly animal.

**BOTARD.** And you pride yourself on your precise thinking.
The rhinoceros, my dear young lady –

**PAPILLON**. There's no need to start a lecture on the rhinoceros here. We're not in school.

**BOTARD**. That's a pity.

**PAPILLON**. *(Turning to* **DAISY**.*)* Well, it's gone nine, Miss Daisy – put the time sheets away. Too bad about the late-comers.

> *(He laughs and turns to the others to continue the discussion.)*

> *(***DAISY*** crosses to the table center. ***BERENGER***, unseen by ***PAPILLON***, creeps up the stairs center. He wears his cap, carries his gloves and stick and has a flower in his lapel. The following speeches overlap.)*

**BERENGER**. *(Moving to right of* **DAISY**.*)* Good morning, Miss Daisy. I'm not late, am I?

**BOTARD**. *(To* **DUDARD** *and* **PAPILLON**.*)* I campaign against ignorance wherever I find it –

**DAISY**. *(To* **BERENGER**.*)* Hurry up, Mr. Berenger.

**BOTARD**. – in palace or humble hut.

**DAISY**. *(To* **BERENGER**.*)* Quick! Sign the time sheet.

> *(She goes to the hat stand and collects* **BERENGER***'s overall.)*

**BERENGER**. *(Signing the time sheet.)* Oh, thank you. Has the boss arrived?

> *(He removes his cap.)*

**DAISY**. *(Moving to left of* **BERENGER** *and taking his cap, gloves and stick.)* Shh! Yes, he's here.

**BERENGER**. Here already?

**BOTARD**. No matter where. Even in printing offices.

**PAPILLON**. Mr. Botard, I consider –

**BERENGER**. *(Removing his jacket.)* But it's not ten past.

> *(He hands the jacket to* **DAISY** *and takes his overall from her.)*

**PAPILLON**. – I consider you have gone too far.

**DUDARD.** I think so, too, sir.

> (**BERENGER** *takes the flower from the lapel of his jacket and gives it to* **DAISY**.)

**PAPILLON.** *(To* **BOTARD**.*)* Are you suggesting that Mr. Dudard, my colleague and yours, a law graduate and a first-class employee, is – ignorant?

> (**DAISY**, *to leave her hands free while she hangs* **BERENGER**'s *jacket etc. on the hat stand, puts the flower in her mouth.* **BERENGER** *faces up center and dons his overall.*)

**BOTARD.** I wouldn't go so far as to say that, but the teaching you get at the university isn't up to what you get at the ordinary schools.

**PAPILLON.** *(Turning to* **DAISY**.*)* What about that time sheet?

**DAISY.** *(Rushing to the table center and picking up the time sheets.)* Here it is, sir.

> (*As she gives* **PAPILLON** *the sheets she realizes about the flower in her mouth and removes it.* **PAPILLON** *does a "take" and crosses to left center.* **DAISY** *smiles archly, goes to her table left and sits.*)

**BERENGER.** *(Moving above the table right.)* Good morning, Mr. Papillon.

**BOTARD.** *(To* **DUDARD**.*)* There is no clear thinking at the universities.

**DUDARD.** *(Moving to the table center.)* Oh, come now!

**BERENGER.** Sorry I was almost late.

> (*He collects his protective sleeves from the shelves right.*)

Morning, Dudard. Morning, Mr. Botard.

**PAPILLON.** Well, Berenger, did you see the rhinoceros by any chance?

**BOTARD.** *(Rising, crossing below the table right to right of* **DUDARD** *and digging him in the ribs.)* All you get at the universities are effete intellectuals with no practical knowledge of life.

**DUDARD**. *(Sitting above the table center.)* Rubbish!

**BERENGER**. *(To* **PAPILLON**; *in a natural tone.)* Oh, yes, I saw it, all right.

> *(He puts on his protective sleeves.)*

**BOTARD**. Pfff!

**DAISY**. So you see, I'm not mad after all.

**BOTARD**. *(Crossing below the table center to left of it; ironically.)* Oh, Mr. Berenger says that out of chivalry – he's a very chivalrous man even if he doesn't look it.

**DUDARD**. What's chivalrous about saying you've seen a rhinoceros?

**BOTARD**. *(Bending and speaking close to* **DUDARD**'*s left ear.)* A lot – when it's said to bolster up a fantastic statement by Miss Daisy.

> *(***DUDARD*** *reacts, then takes out his cigarettes and lighter and lights a cigarette.)*

Everybody is chivalrous to Miss Daisy, it's very understandable.

**PAPILLON**. Don't twist the facts, Mr. Botard. Mr. Berenger took no part in the argument. He's only just arrived.

> *(***PAPILLON*** *exits left, taking the time sheets with him.)*

**BERENGER**. *(Crossing to* **DAISY**.*)* But you did see it, didn't you? We both did.

> *(He picks up a pencil and sharpener from* **DAISY**'*s table.)*

**BOTARD**. Pfff! It's possible that Mr. Berenger thought he saw a rhinoceros.

> *(He makes a gesture behind* **BERENGER**'*s back to indicate he drinks.)*

He's got such a vivid imagination. Anything's possible with him.

*(He crosses and sits right of the table right.)*

**BERENGER.** *(Sharpening the pencil.)* I wasn't alone when I saw the rhinoceros. Or perhaps there were two rhinoceroses.

**BOTARD.** He doesn't even know how many he saw.

**BERENGER.** I was with my friend Jean. And other people were there, too.

**BOTARD.** I don't think you know what you're talking about.

**DAISY.** It was a unicorned rhinoceros.

**BOTARD.** Pfff! They're in league, the two of them, to have us on.

> *(**PAPILLON** enters left, carrying a letter which he gives to **DAISY**. He turns to go but is stopped by the discussion.)*

**DUDARD.** *(To **DAISY**.)* I rather think it had two horns, from what I've heard.

**BOTARD.** You'd better make up your minds.

**PAPILLON.** That will do, gentlemen, time's getting on.

**BOTARD.** Did you see one rhinoceros, Mr. Berenger, or two rhinoceroses?

**BERENGER.** Well, it's hard to say.

**BOTARD.** You don't know. Miss Daisy saw one unicorned rhinoceros. What about your rhinoceros, Mr. Berenger, if indeed there was one, did it have one horn or two?

**BERENGER.** Exactly, that's the whole problem.

**BOTARD.** And it's all very dubious.

**DAISY.** Oh!

**BOTARD.** I don't mean to be offensive. But I don't believe a word of it. No rhinoceros has ever been seen in this country.

**DAISY.** There's a first time for everything.

**BOTARD.** It has never been seen. Except in schoolbook illustrations. Your rhinoceroses are a flower of some journalist's imagination.

**BERENGER.** The word "flower" applied to a rhinoceros seems a bit out of place.

*(He puts the sharpener on* **DAISY***'s table.* **DAISY** *laughs.)*

**DUDARD.** Very true.

**BOTARD.** Your rhinoceros is a myth.

**DAISY.** A myth?

**PAPILLON.** Gentlemen, I think it is high time we started to work.

*(***BERENGER** *crosses above the table right.)*

**BOTARD.** *(To* **DAISY***.)* A myth – like flying saucers.

**DUDARD.** *(Rising and moving right center.)* But nevertheless a cat was trampled to death – that you can't deny.

**BERENGER.** *(Sitting above the table right.)* I was a witness to that.

**DUDARD.** *(Pointing to* **BERENGER***.)* In front of witnesses.

**BOTARD.** Yes, and what a witness!

**PAPILLON.** *(Moving center.)* Gentlemen, gentlemen!

**BOTARD.** *(To* **DUDARD***.)* An example of collective psychosis, Mr. Dudard. Just like religion – the opiate of the people.

**DAISY.** Well, I believe flying saucers exist.

**BOTARD.** Pfff.

**PAPILLON.** *(Firmly.)* That's quite enough. There's been enough gossip. Rhinoceros or no rhinoceros, saucers or no saucers, work must go on. You're not paid to waste your time arguing about animals, real or imaginary.

**BOTARD.** Imaginary!

**DUDARD.** Real!

*(He moves and sits above the table center.)*

**DAISY.** Very real!

**PAPILLON.** *(Crossing to right center.)* Gentlemen, I remind you once again that we are in working hours. I am putting an end to this futile discussion.

**BOTARD.** *(Rising and bowing; wounded and ironic.)* Very well, Mr. Papillon. You are the chief. Your wishes are our commands.

> *(He resumes his seat.)*

**PAPILLON.** Get on, gentlemen. I don't want to be forced to make a deduction from your salaries.

> *(He turns to* **DUDARD.***)*

Mr. Dudard, how is your report on the alcoholic repression law coming along?

**DUDARD.** I'm just finishing it off, sir.

**PAPILLON.** Then do so. It's very urgent.

> *(He turns.)*

Mr. Berenger and Mr. Botard, have you finished correcting the proofs for the wine trade control regulations?

**BERENGER.** Not yet, Mr. Papillon. But they're well on the way.

**PAPILLON.** Then finish off the corrections together. The printers are waiting.

> *(He crosses to left center.)*

And, Miss Daisy, you bring the letters to my office for signature. Hurry up and get them typed.

**DAISY.** Very good, Mr. Papillon.

**PAPILLON.** I shall see you shortly, gentlemen.

> *(***PAPILLON*** exits left, banging the door loudly behind him. There is a long silence as the others settle to work.* **DAISY** *types.* **DUDARD** *works and smokes.* **BOTARD** *seems in a bad temper.* **BERENGER** *is passive and limp. He spreads the proofs on the table in front of him and passes the manuscript to* **BOTARD.** **BERENGER** *reads and corrects the proofs whilst* **BOTARD** *checks the manuscript with a pencil.)*

**BERENGER**. "Laws relating to the control of proprietary wine produce." *(He corrects.)* Control with one L. *(He corrects.)* Proprietary – one P – proprietary. *(He reads.)* "The controlled wines of the Bordeaux region, the lower sections of the upper slopes –"

**BOTARD**. I haven't got that. You've skipped a line.

**BERENGER**. I'll start again. "The Wine Control."

**DUDARD**. Please don't read so loud. I can't concentrate with you shouting at the tops of your voices.

> *(**BERENGER** reads in a whisper, then as he makes some corrections, **BOTARD** resumes his discussion with **DUDARD**.)*

**BOTARD**. It's all a hoax.

**DUDARD**. What's all a hoax?

**BOTARD**. Your rhinoceros business, of course. You've been making all this propaganda to get these rumors started.

**DUDARD**. What propaganda?

> *(**DAISY** stops typing.)*

**BERENGER**. *(Breaking in.)* No question of propaganda.

**DAISY**. Do I have to tell you again, I saw it – I actually saw it, and others did, too.

**DUDARD**. *(To **BOTARD**.)* You make me laugh! Propaganda! Propaganda for what?

**BOTARD**. Oh, you know more about that than I do. Don't make out you're so innocent.

**DUDARD**. *(Rising and moving right center; angrily.)* At any rate, Mr. Botard, I'm not in the pay of any furtive underground organization.

**BOTARD**. *(Rising; angrily.)* That's an insult – I'm not standing for that.

**BERENGER**. *(Rising and trying to calm **BOTARD**; pleadingly.)* Now, now, Mr. Botard –

**DAISY**. *(Rising and rushing to **DUDARD**.)* Now, now, Mr. Dudard –

**BOTARD**. I tell you it's an insult.

(**PAPILLON** *enters suddenly left and crosses to left center. He carries a time sheet.* **BOTARD** *and* **DUDARD** *resume their seats. There is a silence.*)

**PAPILLON.** *(Consulting the time sheet.)* Is Mr. Bœuf not in today?

**BERENGER.** *(Half-looking under his stool.)* No, he isn't. He must be absent.

(*He moves upstage center and opens the windows and shutters.*)

**PAPILLON.** Just when I needed him. *(To* **DAISY**.*)* Did he let anyone know he was ill or couldn't come in?

**DAISY.** He didn't say anything to me.

**PAPILLON.** If this goes on I shall fire him. It's not the first time. Up to now I haven't said anything, but it's not going on like this. Has anyone got the key to his drawer?

(**MRS. BŒUF** *enters up the stairs center. She is a large woman of some forty to fifty years old. She is tearful, breathless, and apprehensive.*)

**BERENGER.** Oh, here's Mrs. Bœuf, Daisy.

(*Right of* **MRS. BŒUF**.*)*

Morning, Mrs. Bœuf.

**MRS. BŒUF.** Morning, Mr. Papillon. Good morning, everyone.

**PAPILLON.** *(Left of* **MRS. BŒUF**.*)* Well, where's your husband? What's happened to him? Is it too much trouble for him to come any more?

**MRS. BŒUF.** *(Breathless.)* Please excuse him – my husband, I mean – he went to visit his family for the weekend. He's got a touch of flu.

**PAPILLON.** So he's got a touch of flu, has he?

**MRS. BŒUF.** *(Handing a telegram to* **PAPILLON**.*)* He says so in the telegram. He hopes to be back on Wednesday.

(*Almost fainting.*)

Could I have a glass of water – and sit down a moment?

*(DUDARD rises and moves his chair slightly right center. BERENGER helps MRS. BŒUF to the chair, into which she flops.)*

PAPILLON. *(To DAISY.)* Give her a glass of water.

DAISY. Yes, straight away.

*(DAISY crosses and exits left.)*

DUDARD. *(To PAPILLON.)* She must have a weak heart.

PAPILLON. *(Moving to left of MRS. BŒUF)* It's a great nuisance that Mr. Bœuf can't come.

*(DAISY enters left, carrying a glass of water. She crosses and hands it to MRS. BŒUF.)*

But that's no reason for you to go to pieces.

MRS. BŒUF. *(With difficulty.)* It's not – it's – well, I was chased here all the way from the house by a rhinoceros.

BERENGER. How many horns did it have?

BOTARD. *(He guffaws. Rising and moving downstage right.)* Don't make me laugh!

DUDARD. *(Indignantly.)* Give her a chance to speak.

*(Cue No. 05: Stairs collapse.)*

MRS. BŒUF. *(Making a great effort to be exact, and pointing in the direction of the stairs center.)* It's down there, by the entrance. It seemed to want to come upstairs.

*(There is a crash from the stairs center. The stairs and rail collapse and a cloud of dust rises. From below an anguished trumpeting is heard.)*

DAISY. My God!

MRS. BŒUF. *(Her hand on her heart; screaming.)* Oh! Ah!

*(She collapses into BERENGER's arms.)*

*(DAISY runs to the door left and fans with it to blow away the dust. PAPILLON rushes to right of the trap and looks down. BOTARD goes above the trap. DUDARD stands below the*

> *trap.* **BERENGER** *administers to* **MRS. BŒUF.**
> *The trumpeting continues.)*

**BERENGER.** *(Patting* **MRS. BŒUF** *cheek.)* Keep calm!

> *(***BOTARD** *and* **DUDARD** *go to the French*
> *windows and fan with them.* **DAISY** *crosses to*
> *left of* **MRS. BŒUF.***)*

**DAISY.** Are you feeling better now, Mrs. Bœuf?

**PAPILLON.** *(Pointing down the stairs.)* There it is! Down there! It is one!

**BOTARD.** *(Moving above the trap.)* I can't see a thing. It's an illusion.

> *(He moves upstage center.)*

**DUDARD.** *(Moving to the trap.)* Of course it's one, down there, turning round and round. It can't get up here. There's no staircase any longer.

**BOTARD.** It's most strange. What can it mean?

**DUDARD.** *(To* **BERENGER.***)* Come and look. Come and have a look at your rhinoceros.

**BERENGER.** I'm coming.

> *(***BERENGER, DAISY, PAPILLON, BOTARD,** *and*
> **DUDARD** *crowd around the trap and look*
> *down.)*

**PAPILLON.** *(To* **BERENGER.***)* You're the rhinoceros expert – take a good look.

**BERENGER.** I'm no rhinoceros expert.

**DAISY.** Oh, look at the way it's going round and round. It looks as if it was in pain – what can it want?

**DUDARD.** It seems to be looking for someone. *(To* **BOTARD.***)* Can you see it now?

**BOTARD.** *(Vexed.)* Yes, yes, I can see it.

**DAISY.** *(To* **PAPILLON.***)* Perhaps we're all seeing things. You as well.

**BOTARD.** I never see things. Something is definitely down there.

**DUDARD.** What do you mean – "something"?

**PAPILLON.** *(Turning to* **BERENGER**.*)* It's obviously a rhinoceros. That's what you saw before, isn't it? *(To* **DAISY**.*)* And you, too?

**DAISY.** Definitely.

**BERENGER.** It's got two horns. It's an African rhinoceros, or Asiatic, rather. Oh, I don't know whether the African rhinoceros has one horn or two.

**PAPILLON.** *(Moving downstage left center.)* It's demolished the staircase – and a good thing, too. When you think how long I've been asking the management to install some steps in place of that worm-eaten old staircase.

**DUDARD.** *(Moving to right of* **PAPILLON**.*)* I sent a report a week ago, Chief.

**PAPILLON.** It was bound to happen, I knew that. I could see it coming, and I was right.

**DAISY.** *(Ironically.)* As always.

**BERENGER.** *(To* **DUDARD** *and* **PAPILLON**.*)* Now look, are two horns a characteristic of the Asiatic rhinoceros or the African? And is one horn a characteristic of the African or the Asiatic one?

**DAISY.** *(Looking down the trap.)* Poor thing, it keeps on trumpeting and going round and round. What does it want? Oh, it's looking at us. *(To the rhinoceros.)* Puss, puss, puss.

**DUDARD.** *(Holding* **DAISY**.*)* I shouldn't try to stroke it, it's probably not tame.

**PAPILLON.** In any case, it's out of reach.

> *(Cue No. 06: The rhinoceros trumpets horribly.)*

**DAISY.** Poor thing!

> *(***BOTARD** *moves downstage right.)*

**BERENGER.** *(To* **BOTARD**; *still insisting.)* You're very well-informed – don't you think that the ones with two horns are –

**PAPILLON.** What are you rambling on about, Berenger? You're a bit under the weather.

**BOTARD** How can it be possible in a civilized country?

**DAISY.** *(To* **BOTARD.***)* All right. But does it exist or not?

**BOTARD.** It's all an infamous plot!

> *(***DUDARD** *crosses to right center. With a political orator's gesture* **BOTARD** *points to* **DUDARD***, quelling him with a look.)*

It's all your fault!

> *(***MRS. BŒUF** *rises and screams.* **BERENGER** *takes* **MRS. BŒUF** *out of the French windows onto the balcony and calms her.)*

**DUDARD.** Why mine, rather than yours?

**BOTARD.** *(Furiously.)* Mine? It's always the little people who get the blame. If I had my way –

**DAISY.** *(Moving to left of* **DUDARD.***)* Calm down, this is no time to quarrel.

**PAPILLON.** *(Moving to left of* **DAISY.***)* We're in a fine mess with no staircase. It's all the management's fault.

**DAISY.** *(Turning to* **PAPILLON.***)* Maybe.

> *(***MRS. BŒUF** *moves below the trap.* **BERENGER** *follows and stands left of the trap.)*

But how are we going to get down?

**PAPILLON.** *(Joking amorously and caressing* **DAISY***'s cheek.)* I'll take you in my arms and we'll float down together.

**DAISY.** *(Rejecting* **PAPILLON***'s advances.)* You keep your horny hands off my face, you old pachyderm.

**PAPILLON.** I was only joking.

> *(The rhinoceros continues its trumpeting. For a few moments* **MRS. BŒUF** *stares fixedly down the trap, then suddenly she lets out a terrible cry.)*

**MRS. BŒUF.** My God! It can't be true!

*(DAISY and DUDARD run above the trap.*
*PAPILLON moves to left of MRS. BŒUF. BOTARD*
*moves to right of the trap.)*

**BERENGER.** What's the matter?

**MRS. BŒUF.** It's my husband! Oh, Bœuf, my poor Bœuf, what's happened to you?

**DAISY.** Are you positive?

**MRS. BŒUF.** I recognize him, I recognize him.

*(Cue No. 07: The rhinoceros replies with a*
*violent but tender trumpeting.)*

**PAPILLON.** Well, that's the last straw! This time he's fired for good.

**DUDARD.** Is he insured?

**BOTARD.** *(Moving down right; aside.)* I understand it all now.

**DAISY.** How can you collect insurance in a case like this?

**MRS. BŒUF.** *(Fainting into BERENGER's arms.)* Oh, my God!

**BERENGER.** Oh!

**DAISY.** Carry her over here.

*(She points to her chair left.)*

*(PAPILLON and BERENGER stagger with*
*MRS. BŒUF to the chair left and set her in it.*
*BERENGER works on MRS. BŒUF and pats her*
*cheeks. DAISY fans her with a notebook.)*

**DUDARD.** Don't upset yourself, Mrs. Bœuf.

*(He moves downstage right of the trap.)*

**MRS. BŒUF.** Ah! Oh!

**DAISY.** Maybe it can all be put right.

**PAPILLON.** *(Moving to left of DUDARD.)* Legally, what can be done?

**DUDARD.** You need to get a solicitor's advice.

**BOTARD.** *(Raising his hands to heaven.)* It's the sheerest madness. What a society!

(*He crosses upstage center.*)

**BOTARD.** You can be certain of one thing – I shall report this to my union. I don't desert a colleague in the hour of need. It won't be hushed up.

**MRS. BŒUF.** (*Coming to.*) My poor darling, I can't leave him like that, my poor darling.

(*Cue No. 08: The trumpeting continues.*)

He's calling me. (*Tenderly.*) He's calling me.

(*She rises and moves to the trap.*)

**DAISY.** Feeling better now, Mrs. Bœuf?

**DUDARD.** She's picking up a bit.

**BOTARD.** (*To* **MRS. BŒUF.**) You can count on the union's support. Would you like to become a member of the committee?

**PAPILLON.** Work's going to be delayed again. What about the post, Miss Daisy?

**DAISY.** I want to know first how we're going to get out of here.

**PAPILLON.** Through the window.

(**DUDARD** *and* **DAISY** *move and look out of the window.* **MRS. BŒUF** *returns to her chair and slumps into it.*)

**BOTARD.** I know where it came from.

**DAISY.** It's too high.

**BERENGER.** Perhaps we ought to call the firemen, and get them to bring ladders.

**PAPILLON.** Miss Daisy, go to my office and telephone the fire brigade.

(**DAISY** *exits left.*)

**MRS. BŒUF.** (*Rising suddenly.*) I can't desert him, I can't desert him now.

**DAISY.** (*Off; into the telephone.*) Hello, hello, is that the fire brigade?

**PAPILLON.** If you want to divorce him – you'd be perfectly justified.

*(PAPILLON crosses and exits left. DAISY enters left holding a telephone receiver, and carries on an inaudible conversation into the telephone.)*

**DUDARD.** You'd be the injured party.

**MRS. BŒUF.** No! Poor thing! This is not the moment for that. I won't abandon my husband in such a state.

**BOTARD.** You're a good woman.

**DUDARD.** *(To MRS. BŒUF.)* But what are you going to do?

*(MRS. BŒUF runs to the table center and puts down her handbag.)*

**BERENGER.** Watch out!

**MRS. BŒUF.** *(Moving to the edge of the trap.)* I can't leave him, I can't leave him now.

**DUDARD.** Hold her back.

*(BERENGER grabs hold of MRS. BŒUF's coat.)*

**DAISY.** *(Calling.)* Mr. Papillon.

**MRS. BŒUF.** I'm taking him home.

**PAPILLON.** *(He enters left.)* What's she trying to do?

**MRS. BŒUF.** *(Preparing to jump into the trap.)* I'm coming, my darling, I'm coming.

**BERENGER.** She's going to jump.

**BOTARD.** It's no more than her duty.

**DUDARD.** She can't do that.

*(MRS. BŒUF jumps down the trap. BERENGER, who tries to restrain her, is left with her coat in his hand. DAISY exits left to replace the telephone.)*

**BERENGER.** I couldn't hold her back.

*(Cue No. 09: The rhinoceros is heard from below, tenderly trumpeting.)*

**MRS. BŒUF.** *(Offstage.)* Here I am, my sweet, I'm here now.

*(DUDARD, BERENGER and PAPILLON look into the trap.)*

**DUDARD.** She landed on his back in the saddle.

**BOTARD.** *(He moves to the trap.)* She's a good rider.

**MRS. BŒUF.** *(Offstage.)* Home now, dear, let's go home.

> *(Cue No. 06: The rhinoceros gallops off.)*

> (**BOTARD** *and* **BERENGER** *rush to the window.)*

**DUDARD.** They're off at a gallop.

> *(The trumpeting ceases and the sound of heavy galloping is heard, fading into the distance.)*

**BERENGER.** They're moving fast.

**DUDARD.** *(To **PAPILLON**.)* Ever done any riding?

**PAPILLON.** A bit – a long time ago.

> *(He looks toward the door left.)*

Is she on the telephone?

**BERENGER.** *(Looking out of the window.)* They're already a long way off. They're out of sight.

**DAISY.** *(She enters left.)* I had trouble getting the firemen.

**BOTARD.** *(Moving downstage right; as if concluding an interior monologue.)* A fine state of affairs.

**DAISY.** I had trouble getting the firemen.

**PAPILLON.** Are there fires all over the place, then?

**BERENGER.** *(Still clutching **MRS. BŒUF**'s coat.)* I agree with Mr. Botard.

> *(He moves right center.)*

Mrs. Bœuf's attitude is very moving; she's a woman of feeling.

**PAPILLON.** *(Sitting on the stool above the table right.)* It means one employee less, who has to be replaced.

> (**DUDARD** *stands right of* **PAPILLON BERENGER** *stands right of the trap.* **DAISY** *is left center* **BOTARD** *is downstage right.)*

**BERENGER.** Do you really think he's no use to us any more?

**DAISY.** No, there aren't any fires, the firemen have been called out for other rhinoceroses.

**BERENGER**. For other rhinoceroses?

**DUDARD & BOTARD**. Other rhinoceroses?

**DAISY**. Yes, other rhinoceroses. They've been reported all over the town. This morning there were seven, now there are seventeen.

**BOTARD**. What did I tell you?

**DAISY**. As many as thirty-two have been reported. They're not official yet, but they're bound to be confirmed soon.

**BOTARD**. *(Less certain.)* Pfff! They always exaggerate.

**PAPILLON**. Are they coming to get us out of here?

**BERENGER**. I'm hungry.

**DAISY**. Yes, they're coming – the firemen are on the way.

> (**BERENGER** *crosses to the hat stand, removes his overall and puts on his jacket.* **DAISY** *covers her typewriter and tidies her papers.)*

**PAPILLON**. What about the work?

**DUDARD**. It looks as if it's out of our hands.

**PAPILLON**. We'll have to make up the lost time.

**DUDARD**. *(Moving to left of* **BOTARD**.*)* Well, Mr. Botard, do you still deny all rhinocerotic evidence?

**BOTARD**. *(Moving to left of* **PAPILLON**.*)* Our union is against your dismissing Mr. Bœuf without notice.

**PAPILLON**. It's not up to me; we shall see what conclusions they reach at the enquiry.

**BOTARD**. *(To* **DUDARD**.*)* No, Mr. Dudard, I do not deny the rhinocerotic evidence. I never have.

**DUDARD**. That's not true.

**DAISY**. Oh, no, that's not true.

**BOTARD**. *(Moving upstage center.)* I repeat I have never denied it. I just wanted to find out exactly where it was all leading. Because I know my own mind. I'm not content to simply state that a phenomenon exists. I make it my business to understand and explain it. At least I could explain it if –

**DUDARD**. Then explain it to us.

**DAISY**. Yes, explain it, Mr. Botard.

**PAPILLON**. Explain it, when your colleagues ask you.

**BOTARD**. I will explain it.

**DUDARD**. We're all listening.

**DAISY**. I'm most curious.

**BOTARD**. I will explain it – one day.

**DUDARD**. Why not now?

**BOTARD**. *(To* **MR. PAPILLON***; menacingly.)* We'll go into the explanation later, in private. *(To the others.)* I know the whys and the wherefores of this whole business.

**DAISY**. What whys?

**BERENGER**. What wherefores?

**DUDARD**. I'd give a lot to know these whys and wherefores.

> *(***BOTARD*** moves downstage left, bringing* **BERENGER** *and* **DAISY** *with him.)*

**BOTARD**. *(With a terrible air; whispering.)* And I also know the names of those responsible. The names of the traitors. You can't fool me. I'll expose the purpose and the meaning of this whole plot. I'll unmask the perpetrators.

**BERENGER**. But who'd want to – ?

**DUDARD**. *(To* **BOTARD**.*)* You're evading the question, Mr. Botard.

**PAPILLON**. Let's have no evasions.

**BOTARD**. Evading? What – me?

**DAISY**. Just now you accused us of suffering from hallucinations.

**BOTARD**. Just now, yes. Now the hallucination has become a provocation.

**DUDARD**. And how do you consider this change came about?

> *(Cue No. 07: Fire engine.)*

**BOTARD**. It's an open secret, gentlemen. Even the man in the street knows about it. Only hyprocrites pretend not to understand.

*(The sound of a fire engine arriving and stopping is heard off.* **PAPILLON** *rises.)*

**DAISY.** *(Running to the window.)* That's the firemen.

*(***BERENGER*** *follows* **DAISY** *to the window.)*

*(Hold sound in background to end of scene.)*

**BOTARD.** *(Removing his overall.)* There's going to be some big changes made; they won't get away with it as easily as that.

*(He crosses and hangs his overall on the hat-stand.)*

**DUDARD.** That doesn't mean anything, Mr. Botard. The rhinoceroses exist, and that's that. That's all there is to it.

**DAISY.** *(Calling over the balcony.)* Up here, firemen.

**FIREMEN.** *(Offstage.)* Put up the ladder.

**BOTARD.** *(To* **DUDARD.***)* I hold the key to all these happenings, an infallible system of interpretation.

**PAPILLON.** I want you all back in the office this afternoon.

*(The top of the* **FIREMAN***'s ladder appears over the balcony.)*

**BOTARD.** *(Putting on his jacket.)* Too bad about the office, Mr. Papillon.

**PAPILLON.** I don't know what the management will say.

**DUDARD.** These are exceptional circumstances.

**BOTARD.** *(Pointing to the window.)* They can't force us to come back this way. We'll have to wait till the staircase is repaired.

**DUDARD.** If anyone breaks a leg, it'll be the management's responsibility.

**PAPILLON.** That's true.

*(The* **FIREMAN** *appears on the ladder.)*

**BERENGER.** After you, Miss Daisy.

**FIREMEN.** Come on, miss.

**DUDARD**. Goodbye, Miss Daisy. See you soon.

> *(The* **FIREMAN** *takes* **DAISY** *in his arms. She gets over the balcony rail and disappears down the ladder with the* **FIREMAN**. **PAPILLON** *moves to the window.)*

**DAISY**. *(As she goes.)* See you soon. Goodbye.

**PAPILLON**. Telephone me tomorrow morning, Miss Daisy. You can come and type the letters at my house. Mr. Berenger, I draw your attention to the fact that we are not on holiday, and that work will resume as soon as possible. *(To* **DUDARD** *and* **BOTARD**.*)* You hear what I say, gentlemen?

**DUDARD**. Of course, Mr. Papillon.

**BOTARD**. They'll go on exploiting us till we drop, of course.

> *(The* **FIREMAN** *appears at the balcony rail.)*

**FIREMAN**. Who's next?

**PAPILLON**. *(To the others.)* Go on.

**DUDARD**. After you, Mr. Papillon.

**BERENGER**. After you, Chief.

**BOTARD**. You first, naturally.

> *(***PAPILLON** *bows shortly to each of them.)*

**PAPILLON**. *(To* **BERENGER**.*)* Bring me Miss Daisy's letters. There, on the desk.

> *(***BERENGER** *collects the papers and letters from the desk left and hands them to* **PAPILLON**.*)*

**FIREMAN**. Come on, hurry up. We've not got all day. We've got others calls to make.

**BOTARD**. What did I tell you?

> *(***PAPILLON** *gets astride the balcony rail. The* **FIREMAN** *gets hold of* **PAPILLON**.*)*

**PAPILLON**. *(To the* **FIREMAN**.*)* Careful of the documents.

> *(The* **FIREMAN** *releases* **PAPILLON**, *takes the letters and disappears.)*

Goodbye, gentlemen.

**DUDARD**. Goodbye, Mr. Papillon.

**BERENGER**. Goodbye, Mr. Papillon.

(**PAPILLON** *disappears down the ladder.*)

**PAPILLON**. *(Offstage.)* Careful of my papers. *(He calls.)*

**DUDARD**. Lock up the offices.

**DUDARD**. *(Calling.)* Don't you worry, Mr. Papillon. *(To* **BOTARD**.*)* After you, Mr. Botard.

**BOTARD**. I am about to descend, gentlemen. And I am going to take this matter up immediately with the proper authorities.

(*He moves on to the balcony.*)

I'll get to the bottom of this so-called mystery.

**DUDARD**. I thought it was all perfectly clear to you.

**BOTARD**. Your irony doesn't affect me. What I'm after are the proofs and the documents – yes, proof positive of your treason.

(*He climbs over the balcony.*)

(*Ironic cheers are heard from a crowd at the foot of the ladder.*)

**DUDARD**. That's absurd.

**BOTARD**. Your insults –

**DUDARD**. *(Interrupting.)* It's you who are insulting me.

**BOTARD**. I don't insult. I merely prove.

(**BOTARD** *disappears down the ladder.*)

**FIREMAN**. *(Off; calling.)* Come on, there.

**DUDARD**. *(To* **BERENGER**.*)* What are you doing this afternoon? Shall we meet for a drink?

**BERENGER**. Sorry, I can't. I'm taking advantage of this afternoon off to go and see my friend Jean. I do want to make it up with him, after all. We got carried away. It was all my fault.

(*The* **FIREMAN** *appears at the balcony rail.*)

**FIREMAN**. Come along, there.

BERENGER. *(To* DUDARD.*)* After you.

DUDARD. After you.

BERENGER. Oh, no, after you.

DUDARD. No, I insist, after you.

BERENGER. No, please, after you, after you.

FIREMAN. Hurry up!

DUDARD. *(To* BERENGER.*)* After you, after you.

BERENGER. No, after you, after you.

*(Sound out.)*

*(*DUDARD *and* BERENGER *climb on to the balcony rail. The crowd cheers as:)*

*(The curtain falls.)*

# ACT II

*(SCENE:* JEAN*'s room. The afternoon of the same day. The door to the entrance hall is downstage left, there is a door upstage right leading to the bathroom and there is a window upstage left. A single divan bed is across the back wall. A chest of drawers stands downstage right. An armchair is left center with a small table downstage left of it. An upright chair is against the wall above the door left. There is a telephone on the chest of drawers. At night the room is lit by a chandelier pendant center with the switch below the door left.)*

*(AT RISE: The window curtains are closed and the room is in semi-darkness.* JEAN *is in bed, lying under the blanket, his back to the audience. He wears pajamas. He coughs. After a few moments there is a knock on the door left.* JEAN *does not answer. The knock is repeated.)*

**BERENGER.** *(Offstage left.)* Jean! *(He knocks.)* Jean!

**JEAN.** *(In a hoarse voice.)* What is it?

**BERENGER.** *(Offstage.)* I've dropped in to see you, Jean.

**JEAN.** Who is it?

**BERENGER.** *(Offstage.)* It's me – Berenger. I hope I'm not disturbing you.

**JEAN.** Oh, it's you, is it? Come in!

**BERENGER.** *(Trying the door.)* The door's locked.

**JEAN.** Just a moment. Oh dear, dear...

*(He gets up in a pretty bad temper. He is wearing green pajamas, his hair is tousled.)*

**JEAN**. Just a moment.

*(He unlocks the door.)*

Just a moment.

*(He goes back to bed, gets under the blanket.)*

Come in!

*(**BERENGER** enters left and switches on the lights.)*

**BERENGER**. Hallo, Jean.

**JEAN**. What time is it? Aren't you at the office?

**BERENGER**. You're still in bed; you're not at the office, then?

*(He goes to the foot of the bed.)*

**JEAN**. *(Still with his back turned.)* Funny, I didn't recognize your voice.

**BERENGER**. I didn't recognize yours, either.

**JEAN**. Sit down.

*(**BERENGER** puts his cap, gloves and stick on the table left center, picks up a box containing a chest expander from the armchair left center and sits in the chair with the box on his lap. **JEAN** coughs.)*

**BERENGER**. You know, Jean, it was stupid of me to get so upset yesterday over a thing like that.

**JEAN**. A thing like what?

**BERENGER**. Yesterday.

**JEAN**. When yesterday? Where yesterday?

**BERENGER**. Don't you remember? It was about that wretched rhinoceros.

**JEAN**. What rhinoceros?

**BERENGER**. The rhinoceros, or rather, the two wretched rhinoceroses we saw.

**JEAN**. Oh, yes, I remember. How do you know they were wretched?

**BERENGER.** Oh, I just said that.

> *(He picks up a magazine from the table.)*

**JEAN.** Oh. Well, let's not talk any more about it.

**BERENGER.** That's very nice of you.

**JEAN.** Then that's that.

**BERENGER.** But I would like to say how sorry I am for being so insistent – and so obstinate – and getting so angry. In fact – I acted stupidly.

**JEAN.** That's not surprising with you.

**BERENGER.** I'm very sorry.

**JEAN.** *(After a pause.)* I don't feel very well.

> *(He coughs.)*

**BERENGER.** That's probably why you're in bed.

> *(He puts the magazine on the table. With a change of tone.)*

You know, Jean, as it turned out, we were both right.

> *(He opens the box and plays with the chest expander.)*

**JEAN.** What about?

**BERENGER.** About – well, you know, the same thing. Sorry to bring it up again, but I'll only mention it briefly. I just wanted you to know that in our different ways we were both right. It's been proved now. There are some rhinoceroses in the town with two horns and some with one.

> *(He accidentally breaks a strand of the chest expander.)*

**JEAN.** That's what I told you. Well, that's just too bad.

**BERENGER.** Yes, too bad.

**JEAN.** Or maybe it's all *to* the good; it depends.

**BERENGER.** *(Bundling the expander into the box.)* In the final analysis it doesn't much matter which comes from where. The important thing, as I see it, is the fact that they're there at all, because...

*(He hides the expander under his chair.)*

**JEAN.** *(He turns, sits up and faces* **BERENGER**.*)* I don't feel well, I don't feel well at all.

**BERENGER.** Oh, I am sorry. What do you think it is?

**JEAN.** I don't know exactly, there's something wrong somewhere.

**BERENGER.** Do you feel weak?

**JEAN.** Not at all.

*(He gets out of bed and does some "push ups.")*

On the contrary, I feel full of beans.

**BERENGER.** I meant just a passing weakness. It happens to everybody.

**JEAN.** It never happens to me.

**BERENGER.** *(Rising and moving to left of* **JEAN**.*)* Perhaps you're too healthy, then.

*(He unsuccessfully tries some "push ups.")*

Too much energy can be a bad thing. It unsettles the nervous system.

**JEAN.** My nervous system is in perfect order.

*(His voice very gradually becomes more and more hoarse.)*

I'm sound in mind and limb. I come from a long line of...

**BERENGER.** I know you do. Perhaps you've just caught a chill. Have you got a temperature?

**JEAN.** I don't know.

*(He stops pushing, rests on one hand and puts the other to his head.)*

Yes, probably I have a touch of fever. My head aches.

**BERENGER.** Just a slight migraine. Would you like me to leave you alone?

**JEAN.** *(Rising.)* No, stay. You don't worry me.

**BERENGER.** Your voice is hoarse, too.

**JEAN.** *(Doing "knee bends.")* Hoarse?

**BERENGER.** A bit hoarse, yes. That's why I didn't recognize it.

**JEAN.** Why should I be hoarse? My voice hasn't changed; it's yours that's changed.

**BERENGER.** Mine?

**JEAN.** Why not?

**BERENGER.** It's possible. I hadn't noticed.

**JEAN.** I sometimes wonder if you're capable of noticing anything.

> *(He sits on the bed and puts his hand to his forehead.)*

Actually it's my forehead that hurts. I must have given it a knock.

> *(His voice is even hoarser.)*

**BERENGER.** When did you do that?

**JEAN.** I don't know. I don't remember it happening.

**BERENGER.** But it must have hurt you.

**JEAN.** I must have done it while I was asleep.

**BERENGER.** The shock would have woken you up. You must have just dreamed you knocked yourself.

> *(He wanders around the armchair and up to the bed again.)*

**JEAN.** I never dream.

**BERENGER.** Your headache must have come on while you were asleep. You've forgotten you dreamed, or rather you only remember subconsciously.

**JEAN.** *(He lies on his back on the bed and does a "cycling" exercise.)* Subconsciously – me? I'm master of my own thoughts, my mind doesn't wander. I think straight, I always think straight.

**BERENGER.** I know that. I haven't made myself clear.

**JEAN.** Then make yourself clearer.

> *(He sits up on the bed.)*

And you needn't bother to make any of your unpleasant observations to me.

BERENGER. One often has the impression that one has knocked oneself when one has a headache.

> (*He moves to left of* JEAN.)

If you'd really knocked yourself, you'd have a bump.

> (*He leans over* JEAN *and looks closely at his forehead.*)

Oh, you've got one, you do have a bump, in fact.

JEAN. A bump?

BERENGER. Just a tiny one.

JEAN. Where?

BERENGER. (*Pointing to* JEAN's *forehead.*) There. It starts just above your nose.

JEAN. I've no bump. We've never had bumps in my family.

BERENGER. Have you got a mirror?

JEAN. That's the limit!

> (*He touches his forehead.*)

I can feel something.

> (*He rises.*)

I'm going to have a look, in the bathroom.

> (JEAN *exits right. While off, he quickly applies green make-up.*)

(*Off.*) It's true, I have got a bump.

> (BERENGER *moves to the bed and tidies it.* JEAN *enters right. His skin has become greener. He leans against the door.*)

So you see, I did knock myself.

BERENGER. (*Looking up at* JEAN.) You don't look well, your skin is quite green.

JEAN. You seem to delight in saying disagreeable things to me. Have you taken a look at yourself lately?

*(He goes to the chest of drawers for the first aid box, panting as he does so.)*

**BERENGER.** *(Continuing with the bed.)* Forgive me. I didn't mean to upset you.

**JEAN.** *(Now very hoarse.)* That's hard to believe.

**BERENGER.** Your breathing's very heavy. Does your throat hurt?

*(He finishes the bed.)*

If your throat hurts, perhaps it's a touch of quinsy.

**JEAN.** *(Panting.)* Why should I have a touch of quinsy?

**BERENGER.** It's nothing to be ashamed of – I sometimes get it.

*(He crosses to JEAN.)*

Let me feel your pulse.

*(He feels JEAN's pulse.)*

**JEAN.** *(In an even hoarser voice.)* Oh, it'll pass.

**BERENGER.** Your pulse is normal. You needn't get alarmed.

**JEAN.** I'm not alarmed in the slightest – why should I be?

**BERENGER.** You're right. A few days' rest will put you right.

**JEAN.** I've no time to rest.

*(He moves toward the door left.)*

I must go and buy some food.

*(He realizes he is without shoes, moves to the bed, sits and puts on his socks.)*

**BERENGER.** There's not much the matter with you if you're hungry. But even so, you ought to take a few days' rest.

*(He moves and sits right of JEAN on the bed.)*

It's wise to take care. Has the doctor been to see you?

**JEAN.** I don't need a doctor.

**BERENGER.** Oh, but you ought to get the doctor.

**JEAN.** You're not going to get the doctor because I don't want the doctor. I can look after myself.

**BERENGER**. You shouldn't reject medical advice.

**JEAN**. Doctors invent illnesses that don't exist.

**BERENGER**. They do it in good faith – just for the pleasure of looking after people.

**JEAN**. They invent illnesses, they invent them, I tell you.

**BERENGER**. Perhaps they do – but after they invent them they cure them.

**JEAN**. I only have confidence in veterinary surgeons. There!

**BERENGER**. *(Taking* **JEAN***'s right hand and looking at his wrist.)* Your veins look swollen. They're jutting out.

**JEAN**. It's a sign of virility.

**BERENGER**. Of course it's a sign of health and strength. But...

> *(He examines* **JEAN***'s forearm more closely.)*

**JEAN**. *(Violently withdrawing his arm.)* What do you think you're doing? – Scrutinizing me as if I was some strange animal.

**BERENGER**. It's your skin –

**JEAN**. What's my skin got to do with you? I don't go on about your skin, do I?

**BERENGER**. It's just that – it seems to be changing colour all the time. It's going green.

> *(He takes* **JEAN***'s hand.)*

It's hardening as well.

**JEAN**. *(Withdrawing his hand.)* Stop mauling me about. What's the matter with you? You're getting on my nerves.

> *(He rises, moves a step left and stands panting.)*

**BERENGER**. *(To himself.)* Perhaps it's more serious than I thought. *(To* **JEAN**.) We must get the doctor.

> *(He rises and moves to the telephone.)*

**JEAN**. Leave that thing alone.

*(He darts over to* **BERENGER** *and pushes him.*
**BERENGER** *staggers to center.)*

**JEAN.** You mind your own business.

*(He laughs harshly.)*

**BERENGER.** All right. It was for your own good.

**JEAN.** *(Crossing below* **BERENGER** *to left; coughing and breathing noisily.)* I know better than you what's good for me.

**BERENGER.** You're breathing very hard.

**JEAN.** *(Moving restlessly upstage left center.)* One breathes as best one can.

*(He picks up the magazine from the table left center.)*

You don't like the way I breathe, and I don't like the way you breathe.

*(He tears a page from the magazine and eats it.)*

Your breathing's too feeble, you can't even hear it –

*(He crosses downstage right center.)*

It's as if you were going to drop dead any moment.

**BERENGER.** Don't say things like that to me, Jean. You know very well I'm your friend.

**JEAN.** *(Circling* **BERENGER**.*)* There's no such thing as friendship. I don't believe in your friendship.

**BERENGER.** That's a very hurtful thing to say.

**JEAN.** There's nothing for you to get hurt about.

**BERENGER.** My dear Jean –

**JEAN.** I'm not your dear Jean.

*(He paces up and down, right center.)*

**BERENGER.** *(Moving downstage left.)* You're certainly in a very misanthropic mood today.

**JEAN.** *(Trying to scratch his back.)* Yes, I am misanthropic, very misanthropic indeed. I like being misanthropic.

**BERENGER.** *(Moving to* **JEAN** *and scratching his back for him.)* You're probably still angry with me over our silly quarrel yesterday. I admit it was my fault. That's why I came to say I was sorry.

**JEAN.** What quarrel are you talking about?

**BERENGER.** I told you just now. You know, about the rhinoceros.

**JEAN.** *(Not listening to* **BERENGER.**) It's not that I hate people. I'm just indifferent to them – or rather, they disgust me.

> *(He paces up and down, left center, like a wild beast in a cage.)*

And they'd better keep out of my way, or I'll run them down.

> *(He crosses towards* **BERENGER.**)

**BERENGER.** *(Watches* **JEAN,** *stepping aside to avoid him.)* You know very well that I shall never stand in your way.

**JEAN.** *(His voice becoming more and more hoarse.)* I've got one aim in life.

> *(He rushes downstage right.)*

And I'm making straight for it.

**BERENGER.** I'm sure you're right. But I feel you're passing through a moral crisis. You mustn't excite yourself, it's bad for you.

**JEAN.** I felt uncomfortable in my clothes.

> *(He unbuttons his pyjama jacket and flaps it.)*

Now my pyjamas irritate me as well.

**BERENGER.** But whatever's the matter with your skin?

**JEAN.** Can't you leave my skin alone? I certainly wouldn't want to change it for yours.

**BERENGER.** *(He moves to* **JEAN** *and feels his chest.)* It's gone like leather.

**JEAN.** That makes it more solid. It's weatherproof.

**BERENGER.** You're getting greener and greener.

**JEAN.** *(Swinging away center.)* You've got color mania today. You're seeing things, you've been drinking again.

**BERENGER.** I did yesterday, but not today.

**JEAN.** It's the result of all your past debauches.

**BERENGER.** I promised you to turn over a new leaf. I take notice when friends like you give me advice. And I never feel humiliated – on the contrary.

**JEAN.** *(Pacing to the door right.)* I don't care what you feel. Brrr!

**BERENGER.** *(Moving center.)* What did you say?

**JEAN.** I didn't say anything. I just went "Brrr!" because I felt like it.

> *(There is a pause.* **BERENGER** *looks fixedly at* **JEAN.***)*

**BERENGER.** Do you know what's happened to Bœuf? He's turned into a rhinoceros.

**JEAN.** What happened to Bœuf?

**BERENGER.** He's turned into a rhinoceros.

**JEAN.** *(Fanning himself with the flaps of his pyjama jacket.)* Brrr!

**BERENGER.** *(Flapping his jacket and moving to* **JEAN.***)* Come on, now, stop joking.

**JEAN.** *(Turning angrily on* **BERENGER.***)* I can puff if I want to, can't I? I've every right – I'm in my own house.

**BERENGER.** I didn't say you couldn't.

**JEAN.** And I shouldn't if I were you. I feet hot, I feel hot. Brrr! Just a moment. I must cool myself down.

> *(***JEAN** *darts into the bathroom.)*

**BERENGER.** He must have a fever.

> *(The sound of* **JEAN** *puffing and water running from a tap is heard off right.)*

**JEAN.** *(Offstage.)* Brrr!

**BERENGER.** He's got the shivers. I'm jolly well going to phone the doctor.

*(He goes to the telephone and lifts the receiver.)*

**JEAN**. *(Offstage.)* So old Bœuf turned into a rhinoceros, did he? Ah, ah, ah! He was just having you on, he'd disguised himself.

> (**JEAN** *puts his head round the bathroom door. He is very green and has a prominent bump over his nose.)*

He was just disguised.

> (**BERENGER** *hastily replaces the receiver.* **JEAN** *withdraws his head.)*

**BERENGER**. *(Turning and moving towards the bathroom door.)* He looked very serious about it, I assure you.

**JEAN**. *(Offstage.)* Oh, well, that's his business.

**BERENGER**. *(Moving downstage left.)* I'm sure he didn't do it on purpose. He didn't want to change.

**JEAN**. *(Offstage.)* How do you know?

**BERENGER**. Well, everything led one to suppose so.

**JEAN**. *(Offstage.)* And what if he did do it on purpose? Eh? What if he did it on purpose?

**BERENGER**. *(Moving upstage left.)* I'd be very surprised. At any rate, Mrs. Bœuf didn't seem to know about it.

**JEAN**. *(Off; in a very hoarse voice.)* Ah, ah, ah! Fat, old Mrs. Bœuf! She's just a fool!

**BERENGER**. Well, fool or no fool...

> *(He looks out of the window upstage left.)*

> (**JEAN** *enters swiftly from the bathroom. He is without his pyjama jacket and his back and chest are now green.)*

**JEAN**. Bœuf never let his wife know what he was up to.

**BERENGER**. *(His back turned to* **JEAN**.*)* You're wrong there, Jean – it was a very united family.

**JEAN**. Very united, was it? Are you sure? Hum, hum, brrr!

> (**JEAN** *exits to the bathroom.* **BERENGER** *turns and moves center.)*

**BERENGER**. Very united. And the proof is that –

> (**JEAN** *slams the bathroom door shut.*)

**JEAN**. *(Offstage.)* Bœuf led his own private life. He had a secret side to him deep down which he kept to himself.

**BERENGER**. I shouldn't make you talk, it seems to upset you.

**JEAN**. *(Offstage.)* On the contrary, it relaxes me.

**BERENGER**. Even so, let me call the doctor, I beg you.

**JEAN**. *(Offstage.)* I absolutely forbid it. I can't stand obstinate people.

> (**JEAN** *enters from the bathroom. He carries his pyjama jacket and is greener than ever. He speaks only with difficulty and his voice is almost unrecognizable.* **BERENGER** *backs away left, a little scared.* **JEAN** *puts the pyjama jacket on the bed.*)

Well, whether he changed into a rhinoceros on purpose or against his will, he's probably all the better for it.

> (*He moves to the chest of drawers, opens a drawer and scatters the contents on the floor.*)

**BERENGER**. *(Moving right center.)* How can you say a thing like that?

> (*He picks up the shirts etc. from the floor.*)

Surely you don't think – ?

**JEAN**. You always see the black side of everything. It obviously gave him great pleasure to turn into a rhinoceros. There's nothing extraordinary in that.

**BERENGER**. *(Moving and putting the garments on the bed.)* There's nothing extraordinary in it, but I doubt if it gave him much pleasure.

**JEAN**. And why not, pray?

**BERENGER**. It's hard to say exactly why; it's just something you feel.

**JEAN**. I tell you it's not as bad as all that.

> (*He scratches his back on the corner of the open drawer.*)

**JEAN.** After all, rhinoceroses are living creatures the same as us; they've got as much right to life as we have.

**BERENGER.** As long as they don't destroy ours in the process. You must admit the difference in mentality.

**JEAN.** *(Crossing very fast to the window.)* Are you under the impression –

> **(BERENGER** *jumps on to the bed.)*

that our way of life is superior?

**BERENGER.** Well, at any rate, we have our own moral standards which I consider incompatible with the standards of these animals.

**JEAN.** *(Moving left center.)* Moral standards!

> *(He sweeps the books from the table left center on to the floor.)*

I'm sick of moral standards. We need to go beyond moral standards.

> *(He knocks the table over.)*

**BERENGER.** What would you put in their place?

**JEAN.** *(He darts out of the door left and crosses the front of the stage to right center.)* Nature!

**BERENGER.** *(Following* **JEAN** *to the door left.)* Nature?

**JEAN.** Nature has its own laws. Morality's against Nature.

**BERENGER.** Are you suggesting we replace our moral laws by the law of the jungle?

> *(***JEAN** *crosses quickly to the door left and comes into the room.* **BERENGER** *flattens himself against the "fourth wall.")*

**JEAN.** It would suit me, suit me fine.

**BERENGER.** You say that. But deep down, no one –

**JEAN.** *(Moving up left center and jumping on to the bed.)* We've got to build our lives on new foundations. We must get back to primeval integrity.

**BERENGER.** I don't agree with you at all.

**JEAN.** *(Jumping from the bed and moving to the windows; breathing noisily.)* I can't breathe.

**BERENGER.** *(Setting up the table and replacing the books.)* Just think a moment. You must admit that we have a philosophy that animals don't share, and an irreplaceable set of values which it's taken centuries of human civilization to build up.

**JEAN.** *(Crossing to the door right.)* When we've demolished all that, we'll be better off.

(JEAN exits to the bathroom.)

**BERENGER.** I know you don't mean that seriously. You're joking! It's just poetic fancy.

**JEAN.** *(Offstage; almost trumpeting.)* Brrr!

**BERENGER.** I'd never realized you were a poet.

**JEAN.** *(Offstage; trumpeting.)* Brrr!

**BERENGER.** That's not what you believe fundamentally – I know you too well. You know as well as I do that mankind –

**JEAN.** *(Offstage; interrupting.)* Don't talk to me about mankind!

**BERENGER.** I mean the human individual, humanism.

**JEAN.** *(Offstage.)* Humanism is all washed up. You're a ridiculous old sentimentalist.

**BERENGER.** *(Crossing to the bathroom door.)* But you must admit that the mind –

**JEAN.** *(Offstage.)* Just clichés. You're talking rubbish!

**BERENGER.** Rubbish!

**JEAN.** *(Offstage; in a very hoarse voice, difficult to understand.)* Utter rubbish!

**BERENGER.** I'm amazed to hear you say that, Jean, really. You must be out of your mind. You wouldn't like to be a rhinoceros yourself, now would you?

**JEAN.** *(Offstage.)* Why not? I'm not a victim of prejudice like you.

**BERENGER.** Can you speak more clearly? I didn't catch what you said. You swallowed the words.

**JEAN.** *(Offstage.)* Then keep your ears open.

**BERENGER.** What?

JEAN. *(Offstage.)* Keep your ears open. I said, what's wrong with being a rhinoceros? I'm all for change.

BERENGER. It's not like you to say a thing like that –

> *(He stops short. **JEAN** enters from the bathroom. His appearance is truly alarming. He has, in fact, become completely green. The bump on his forehead is practically a rhinoceros horn.)*

*(After a pause.)* Oh, you really must be out of your mind.

> *(He moves quickly to left of the bed. **JEAN** jumps on to the bed, goes on all fours and scrabbles the bed coverings on to the floor, talking in a fast and furious gabble, and making very weird sounds.)*

You mustn't get into such a state – calm down. I hardly recognize you anymore.

JEAN. *(His words hardly distinguishable.)* Hot – far too hot. Demolish the lot, clothes itch, they itch.

> *(He discards his socks.)*

BERENGER. What are you doing? You're not yourself. You're generally so modest.

JEAN. The swamps! The swamps!

BERENGER. Look at me. Can't you see me any longer? Can't you hear me?

JEAN. I can hear you perfectly well. I can see you perfectly well.

> *(He jumps from the bed and lunges toward **BERENGER**, head down.)*

BERENGER. *(Dodging.)* Watch out!

JEAN. *(He charges downstage left. Puffing noisily.)* Sorry!

> *(**JEAN** darts at great speed into the bathroom. **BERENGER** goes toward the door left as if to escape, then changes his mind.)*

**BERENGER**. I really can't leave him like that – after all he is a friend.

> (**BERENGER** *exits to the bathroom.*)

*(Offstage.)* I'm going to get the doctor. It's absolutely necessary, believe me.

**JEAN**. *(Offstage.)* No!

**BERENGER**. *(Offstage.)* Calm down, Jean, you're being ridiculous. Oh, your horn's getting longer and longer – you're a rhinoceros.

**JEAN**. *(Offstage.)* I'll trample you, I'll trample you down.

> *(Cue No. 08: Crash.)*

> *(A lot of noise and trumpeting comes from the bathroom. Some towels and a loofah are thrown violently through the door.* **BERENGER***, very frightened, staggers from the bathroom and closes the door with difficulty against the resistance that is being made from inside.)*

**BERENGER**. *(Pushing against the door.)* He's a rhinoceros, he's a rhinoceros! I never would have thought it of him – never.

> *(A rhinoceros horn pierces the door. He runs to the door left, opens it and calls.)*

There's a rhinoceros in the building! Get the police!

> *(He goes through the doorway and crosses the front of the stage to right.)*

Porter, porter, there's a rhinoceros in the house, get the police! Porter!

> *(He crosses downstage left. A rhinoceros head appears in the corner downstage left trumpeting is heard off.)*

Another!

> *(He runs across the front of the stage to right. A rhinoceros head appears in the corner downstage right.)*

Oh, my God!

*(He runs center.)*

My God! Oh, my God!

*(He looks out front as if from a window.)*

There's a whole herd of them in the street now.

*(He looks around.)*

Where can I get out? Where can I get out? If only they'd keep to the middle of the road. They're all over the pavement as well. Where can I get out? Where can I get out?

*(He runs distractedly into the room, goes to the window upstage left and looks out. The bathroom door continues to shake and* **JEAN** *continues to trumpet and hurl incomprehensible insults.)*

A whole herd of them. And they always said the rhinoceros was a solitary animal! It's not true, that's a conception they'll have to revise! They've smashed up all the public benches.

*(He wrings his hands.)*

What's to be done?

*(A rhinoceros head is thrust through the window.* **BERENGER** *runs center. The bathroom door bursts open and a rhinoceros head appears in the doorway. He yells.)*

Rhinoceros!

*(He jumps on to the bed.)*

Rhinoceros!

*(***BERENGER*** *throws himself against the back wall, which yields; the street is visible in the background. He flees, shouting, as:)*

*(Curtain.)*

# ACT III

*(SCENE:* **BERENGER***'s room. A few days later.
The room bears a striking resemblance to
that of* **JEAN***'s. Only certain details, one or two
extra pieces of furniture, reveal that it is a
different room. The door is left and is covered
by a curtain. A door and an alcove cupboard,
right, are also curtained. There is a window
upstage left.* **BERENGER***'s bed is downstage
right with the head down stage. A small table
with a table lamp and telephone stands by
the head of the bed. A larger table is against
the wall right. There is a chest of drawers
with a radio on it, under the window. A small
cabinet stands above the door left. Three
upright chairs stand left center, right center,
and downstage center. A heavy dining table
is wedged against the door left, upstage right
there is a clothes horse with clothes airing on
it, and across the back of the room there is a
clothes line with shirts etc. drying. A mirror
is presumed to be on the "fourth wall.")*

*(Cue No. 09: Rhino's growl.)*

*(AT RISE: The window curtains are closed
and the room is in semi-darkness.* **BERENGER**
*is lying fully dressed on the bed, with a bottle
of brandy on the floor beside him. His head
is bandaged. He seems to be having a bad
dream, and writhes in his sleep.)*

**BERENGER.** No. *(He pauses.)* Watch out for the horns!

*(He pauses. The sound of a considerable number of rhinoceroses is heard passing under the window upstage left.)*

No.

*(He falls to the floor still fighting with what he has seen in his dream, and wakes up. He rises, switches on the table lamp, puts his hand to his forehead with an apprehensive air, moves downstage center, faces front and looks into an imaginary mirror in the "fourth wall." He lifts the bandage as the rhinoceros noises fade. He heaves a sigh of relief when he sees he has no bump. He hesitates, goes to his bed, lies on it and instantly gets up again. He picks up the bottle and a glass and is about to pour himself a drink, then after a short internal struggle he replaces the bottle and glass and sits on the bed.)*

Now, now, where's your willpower?

*(The rhinoceroses are heard again under the window for a few moments. He rises, moves downstage center, returns to the bed, hesitates a moment, then with a gesture of, "Oh, what's it matter," he pours himself a glass of brandy which he downs at one go. He replaces the bottle and glass. He coughs. His cough seems to worry him; he coughs again and listens hard to the sound. He moves downstage center, opens curtains at an imaginary window in the "fourth wall," then coughs again.)*

No, it's not the same.

*(He calms down, feels his bandaged forehead, goes to his bed, lies on it and seems to fall asleep.)*

*(Sound out. Stop tape.)*

*(There is a knock at the door left. He starts up.)*

What is it?

**DUDARD.** *(Offstage left.)* I've dropped by to see you, Berenger.

**BERENGER.** Who is it?

**DUDARD.** *(Offstage.)* It's me.

**BERENGER.** Who's me?

**DUDARD** *(Offstage.)* Me – Dudard.

**BERENGER.** Ah, it's you. Come in.

**DUDARD.** *(Offstage.)* I hope I'm not disturbing you.

> *(He tries to open the door.)*

The door's locked.

**BERENGER.** *(Sitting up.)* Just a moment. Oh, dear, dear!

> *(He rises, crosses to the door left, moves the table a little, unlocks the door and moves left center. DUDARD enters left.)*

**DUDARD.** Hello, Berenger.

**BERENGER.** Hello, Dudard. What time is it?

**DUDARD.** So, you're still barricaded in your room.

> *(BERENGER and DUDARD carry the table center.)*

Feeling any better, old man?

> *(He sets one chair above the table and one left of it.)*

**BERENGER.** *(Setting a chair right of the table.)* Forgive me, I didn't recognize your voice.

> *(He goes to the window upstage left and opens the curtains.)*

Yes, yes, I think I'm a bit better.

**DUDARD.** My voice hasn't changed. I recognized yours easily enough.

**BERENGER**. *(Very nervous.)* I'm sorry, I thought that... You're right, your voice is quite normal. Mine hasn't changed either – has it?

**DUDARD**. Why should it have changed?

**BERENGER**. *(Taking down the clothes lines.)* I'm not a bit – a bit hoarse, am I?

> *(He puts the washing on the clothes horse and the line in the cupboard right.)*

**DUDARD**. Not that I notice.

**BERENGER**. That's good. That's very reassuring.

**DUDARD**. Why, what's the matter with you?

**BERENGER**. *(Moving center.)* I don't know – does one ever know? Voices can suddenly change – they do change, alas!

**DUDARD**. Have you caught cold, as well?

**BERENGER**. I hope not – I sincerely hope not. But do sit down, Dudard, take a seat.

**DUDARD**. *(Sitting left of the table.)* Are you still feeling a bit off color?

> *(**BERENGER**, fidgety and nervous, moves below the table center. **DUDARD** points to **BERENGER**'s bandage.)*

Is your head still bad?

**BERENGER**. *(Moving above the table.)* Oh, yes, I've still got a headache. But there's no bump, I haven't knocked myself –

> *(He leans over the table with his head close to **DUDARD** and lifts the bandage.)*

– have I?

**DUDARD**. No, there's no bump as far as I can see.

**BERENGER**. *(Moving downstage right.)* I hope there never will be. Never.

**DUDARD**. If you don't knock yourself, why should there be?

**BERENGER**. *(Pacing up and down, right.)* If you really don't want to knock yourself, you don't.

**DUDARD.** Obviously. One just has to take care. But what's the matter with you? You're all nervous and agitated. It must be your migraine.

**BERENGER.** Migraine! Don't talk to me about migraine. Don't talk about them.

**DUDARD.** It's understandable that you've got a migraine after all that emotion.

**BERENGER.** I can't seem to get over it.

**DUDARD.** Then it's not surprising you've got a headache.

**BERENGER.** *(Darting to the imaginary mirror downstage center and lifting the bandage.)* Nothing there. You know, it can all start from something like that.

**DUDARD.** What can all start?

**BERENGER.** I'm frightened of becoming someone else.

**DUDARD.** Calm yourself now, and sit down. Dashing up and down the room like that can only make you more nervous.

**BERENGER.** You're right, I must keep calm.

*(He sits right of the table.)*

I just can't get over it, you know.

**DUDARD.** About Jean, you mean? I know.

**BERENGER.** Yes, Jean, of course – and the others, too.

**DUDARD.** I realize it must have been a shock to you.

**BERENGER.** Well, that's not surprising, you must admit.

**DUDARD.** I suppose so, but you mustn't dramatize the situation; it's no reason for you to –

**BERENGER.** I wonder how you'd have felt. Jean was my best friend. Then to watch him change before my eyes. And the way he got so furious.

*(He rises, moves to the chest of drawers upstage left and picks up a duster.)*

**DUDARD.** I know. You felt let down. I understand. Try and not think about it.

**BERENGER.** *(Moving to the table and dusting it.)* How can I help thinking about it? He was such a warm-hearted person, always so human. Who'd have thought it of him? We'd known each other for – for donkey's years.

*(He collects the tablecloth from upstage center and spreads it on the table.)*

He was the last person I'd have expected to change like that. I felt more sure of him than of myself. And then to do that to me.

**DUDARD**. I'm sure he didn't do it specially to annoy you.

**BERENGER**. *(Dusting the chairs.)* It seemed as if he did. If you'd seen the state he was in – the expression on his face –

**DUDARD**. It's just that you happened to be with him at the time. It would have been the same no matter who was there.

**BERENGER**. *(Replacing the duster on the chest of drawers.)* But after all our years together he might have controlled himself in front of me.

*(He moves center.)*

**DUDARD**. You think everything revolves round you, you think that everything that happens concerns you personally; you're not the center of the universe, you know.

**BERENGER**. Perhaps you're right. I must try to readjust myself, but the phenomenon in itself is so disturbing.

*(He moves upstage left, takes a plant from the chest of drawers and puts it on the table center.)*

It's absolutely shattered me. What can be the reason for it?

**DUDARD**. Up to now I haven't found a satisfactory explanation. I observe the facts, and I digest them.

*(**BERENGER** moves upstage left and dusts the radio.)*

Perhaps he felt an urge for some fresh air, the country, the wide-open spaces – perhaps he felt a need to relax. I'm not saying that's any excuse...

**BERENGER.** I understand what you mean, at least I'm trying to.

*(He crosses to the bed and tidies it.)*

**DUDARD.** Why get upset over a few cases of rhinoceritis? Perhaps it's just another disease.

**BERENGER.** Exactly! And I'm frightened of catching it.

*(He picks up the counterpane and folds it.)*

**DUDARD.** *(Rising.)* Oh, stop thinking about it.

*(He moves about the table.)*

Really, you attach too much importance to the whole business. Jean's case isn't symptomatic – he was far too excitable, a bit wild, an eccentric. You musn't base your judgements on exceptions. It's the average case you must consider.

**BERENGER.** *(Clutching the counterpane to him.)* Yes, you're right.

*(He sits on the bed.)*

He must have been temporarily unbalanced. And yet he gave his reasons for it – he'd obviously given it a lot of thought, and weighed the pros and cons. And what about Bœuf, then, was he mad, too? And what about all the others?

**DUDARD.** You can be sure that Bœuf and the others didn't do what they did – become what they became – just to annoy you.

*(He moves to left of **BERENGER**.)*

They wouldn't have gone to all that trouble.

**BERENGER.** That's true – that makes sense. It's a reassuring thought. Or on the other hand, perhaps that makes it worse.

*(Cue No. 09, continued: Rhinoceroses are heard galloping past the window upstage left.)*

*(He rises.)*

There, you hear that?

**DUDARD.** *(Pushing* **BERENGER** *back onto his seat.)* Oh, why can't you leave them alone! They're not doing you any harm. Really, you're obsessed by them. It's not good for you. You're wearing yourself out. You've had one shock – why look for more? You just concentrate on getting back to normal.

**BERENGER.** I wonder if I really am immune?

**DUDARD.** In any case it's not fatal. Certain illnesses are good for you. Anyway, I'm convinced this is something you can cure if you really want to. They'll get over it, you'll see.

**BERENGER.** But it's bound to have certain after-effects. An organic upheaval like that can't help but leave –

**DUDARD.** They're only temporary, don't you worry.

**BERENGER.** Are you absolutely certain?

**DUDARD.** *(Crossing downstage left.)* I think so, yes, I suppose so.

> *(He removes his spectacles and rubs his forehead.)*

**BERENGER.** But if one really doesn't want to, really doesn't want to catch this thing –

> *(***DUDARD** *moves to the window up left and looks out.)*

which after all is a nervous disease – then you don't catch it, you simply don't catch it.

> *(He switches off the table lamp.)*

Do you feel like a brandy?

> *(He picks up the bottle.)*

**DUDARD.** *(Moving downstage left center.)* Not for me, thank you, I never touch it. But don't mind me if you want some – you go ahead, don't worry about me. But watch out it doesn't make your headache worse.

**BERENGER.** *(He pours a drink for himself.)* Alcohol is good for epidemics. It immunizes you. It kills influenza microbes, for instance.

**DUDARD**. Perhaps it doesn't kill all microbes. They don't know about rhinoceritis yet.

**BERENGER**. Jean never touched alcohol. He just pretended to. Maybe that's why he – perhaps that explains his attitude.

> *(Offering a glass to* **DUDARD**.*)*

You're sure you won't?

**DUDARD**. No, no, never before lunch, thank you.

> *(***BERENGER*** drinks. He coughs, still holding the bottle and glass.)*

You see, you can't take it. It makes you cough.

**BERENGER**. *(Worried.)* Yes, it did make me cough.

> *(He moves to right of the table center.)*

How did I cough?

**DUDARD**. Like everyone coughs when they drink something a bit strong.

**BERENGER**. *(Moving and putting the glass and bottle on the table right center.)* There wasn't anything odd about it, was there? It *was* a real human cough?

**DUDARD**. What are you getting at? It was an ordinary human cough. What other sort of cough could it have been?

**BERENGER**. I don't know. Perhaps an animal's cough. Do rhinoceroses cough?

**DUDARD**. Look, Berenger, you're being ridiculous, you invent difficulties for yourself, you ask yourself the weirdest questions. I remember you said yourself that the best protection against the thing was willpower.

**BERENGER**. Yes, I did.

**DUDARD**. Well, then, prove you've got some.

**BERENGER**. I have, I assure you.

**DUDARD**. Prove it to yourself – now. Don't drink any more brandy. You'll feel more sure of yourself then.

**BERENGER**. You deliberately misunderstand me. The only reason I take it is because it keeps the worst at bay; I'm doing it quite deliberately. When the epidemic's over, then I shall stop drinking. I'd already decided that before the whole business began. I'm just putting it off for the time being.

**DUDARD.** You're inventing excuses for yourself.

**BERENGER.** Do you think I am? In any case, that's got nothing do with what's happening out there.

**DUDARD.** How do we know?

**BERENGER.** *(Alarmed.)* Do you really think so? You think that's how the rot sets in? I'm not an alcoholic.

> *(He moves downstage center, looks in the imaginary mirror and examines his eyes.)*

Do you think by any chance...

> *(He touches his face and pats his bandaged forehead.)*

Nothing's changed; it hasn't done any harm so it must have done good – or it's harmless at any rate.

**DUDARD.** I was only joking. I was just teasing you.

> *(He sits on the table center and toys with the plant.)*

When you've got over your shock completely and you can get out for a breath of fresh air, you'll feel better – you'll see. All these morbid ideas will vanish.

**BERENGER.** Go out? I suppose I'll have to. I'm dreading the moment. I'll be bound to meet some of them.

**DUDARD.** What if you do? They don't attack you. If you leave them alone, they just ignore you. You can't say they're spiteful. They've even got a certain natural innocence, a sort of frankness. Besides, I walked right along the avenue to get here, and I arrived safe and sound, didn't I? No trouble at all.

**BERENGER.** Just the sight of them upsets me. It's a nervous thing.

> *(He moves upstage center.)*

**BERENGER**. I don't get angry – no, it doesn't pay to get angry, you never know where it'll lead to.

*(He moves upstage right of the table center.)*

But it does something to me –

*(He points to his heart.)*

here. I get a tight feeling inside.

**DUDARD**. You've no sense of humor, that's your trouble – none at all. You must learn to be more detached, and try and see the funny side.

**BERENGER**. I feel responsible for everything that happens. I feel involved – I just can't be indifferent.

**DUDARD**. *(Rising and moving left.)* Judge not lest ye be judged. If you start worrying about everything that happens you'd never be able to go on living.

**BERENGER**. *(Sitting right of the table.)* If only it had happened somewhere else, in some other country, and we'd just read about it in the papers, one could discuss it quietly, examine the question from all points of view, and come to an objective conclusion. We could organize debates with professors and writers and lawyers, and bluestockings and artists and people. And the ordinary man in the street, as well – it would be very interesting and instructive. But when you're involved yourself, when you suddenly find yourself up against the brutal facts, you can't help feeling directly concerned – the shock is too violent for you to stay cool and detached. I'm frankly surprised, I'm very, very surprised. I can't get over it.

**DUDARD**. *(Wandering above the table center.)* Well, I'm surprised, too.

*(He fiddles with the plant on the table.)*

Or rather, I was. Now I'm starting to get used to it.

**BERENGER**. Your nervous system is better balanced than mine. You're lucky. But don't you agree it's all very unfortunate –

**DUDARD.** *(Interrupting.)* I don't say it's a good thing. And don't get the idea that I'm on the rhinoceroses' side –

> *(Cue No. 09, continued: Rhinoceroses are heard apparently passing under the window in the "fourth wall.")*

**BERENGER.** *(Jumping up and going to the imaginary window downstage center.)* There they are again, a whole gang of them, rushing up and down the street.

> *(Moving right.)*

I just can't get used to it.

**DUDARD.** *(With a step towards* **BERENGER.***)* But you must – you must face the facts and get over it. This is the situation and you must accept it.

**BERENGER.** *(Sitting on the bed.)* Well, I don't want to accept it.

**DUDARD.** What else can you do? What are your plans?

**BERENGER.** I don't know for the moment. I must think it over. I shall write to the papers; I'll draw up manifestos; I shall apply for an audience with the mayor – or his deputy, if the mayor's too busy.

**DUDARD.** You leave the authorities to act as they think best. I'm not sure if morally you have the right to butt in. In any case, I still think it's not all that serious.

> *(He turns the chair right of the table to face* **BERENGER** *and sits.)*

I consider it's silly to get worked up because a few people decide to change their skins. They just didn't feel happy in the ones they had. They're free to do as they like.

**BERENGER.** We must attack the evil at the roots.

**DUDARD.** The evil! That's just a phrase. Who knows what is evil and what is good? It's just a question of personal preferences. You're worried about your own skin – that's the truth of the matter. But you'll never become a rhinoceros, believe me – you haven't got the vocation.

**BERENGER**. There you are, you see. If our leaders and fellow citizens all think like you, they'll never take any action.

**DUDARD**. You wouldn't want to ask for help from abroad, surely? This is an internal affair, it only concerns our country.

**BERENGER**. I believe in international solidarity.

**DUDARD**. *(Laughing.)* You're a Don Quixote. Oh, I don't mean that nastily, don't be offended. I'm only saying it for your own good, because you really need to calm down.

**BERENGER**. *(After a pause.)* You're right, I know – forgive me. I get too worked up. But I'll change, I will change. I'm sorry to keep you all this time listening to my ramblings. You must have work to do. Did you get my application for sick leave?

**DUDARD**. Don't worry about that. It's all in order. In any case, the office hasn't resumed work.

**BERENGER**. Haven't they repaired the staircase yet? What negligence! That's why everything goes so badly.

**DUDARD**. They're repairing it now. But it's slow work.

*(He rises and replaces the chair right of the table.)*

It's not easy to find workmen. They sign on and work for a couple of days, then don't turn up anymore. Then you have to look for others.

**BERENGER**. And they talk about unemployment. At least I hope we're getting a stone staircase.

**DUDARD**. *(Moving to left of the table.)* No, it's wood again, but new wood this time.

**BERENGER**. Oh, the way these organizations stick to the old routine.

*(He lies on the bed.)*

They chuck money down the drain, but when it's needed for something really useful they pretend they can't afford it. I bet Mr. Papillon's none too pleased. He was dead set on having a stone staircase. What's he say about it?

**DUDARD.** We haven't got a chief any more. Mr. Papillon's resigned.

**BERENGER.** It's not possible!

**DUDARD.** It's true, I assure you.

**BERENGER.** *(Sitting up.)* Well, I'm amazed. Was it on account of the staircase?

**DUDARD.** I don't think so. Anyway that wasn't the reason he gave.

**BERENGER.** What was it then? What got into him?

**DUDARD.** He's retiring to the country.

**BERENGER.** But he's not the age. He might still have become director.

**DUDARD.** He's given it all up. Said he needed a rest.

**BERENGER.** I bet the management's pretty upset to see him go – they'll have to replace him. All your diplomas should come in useful – you stand a good chance.

**DUDARD.** I suppose I might as well tell you – it's really rather funny – the fact is, he turned into a rhinoceros.

> *(Cue No. 09, continues: Rhinoceros noises are heard in the distance.)*

**BERENGER.** *(After a pause.)* A rhinoceros!

> *(He slowly rises.)*

*(Softly.)* Mr. Papillon a rhinoceros! I can't believe it. I don't think it's funny at all.

> *(He moves violently downstage right and turns.)*

Why didn't you tell me before?

**DUDARD.** Well, you know you've no sense of humor. I didn't want to tell you.

> *(He crosses to right center.)*

I didn't want to tell you because I knew very well you wouldn't see the funny side, and it would upset you. You know how impressionable you are.

**BERENGER.** *(Raising his arms to heaven.)* Oh, that's awful. Mr. Papillon! And he had such a good job.

**DUDARD.** *(Crossing to left.)* That proves his metamorphosis was sincere.

**BERENGER.** He couldn't have done it on purpose. He let himself be talked into it, I feel sure.

**DUDARD.** That could happen to anybody.

**BERENGER.** *(Crossing to left center; alarmed and very worried.)* To anybody? Oh, no, not to you it couldn't – could it? And not to me.

**DUDARD.** We must hope not.

**BERENGER.** Because we don't want to – that's so, isn't it? Tell me, that *is* so, isn't it?

**DUDARD.** *(Patting* **BERENGER**'s *shoulder; reassuringly.)* Yes, yes, of course.

**BERENGER.** *(With a nervous laugh, he moves away right center.)* I feel sure that Botard must have taken a very poor view of it – what did he think of his chief's behaviour?

**DUDARD.** Oh, poor old Botard was quite indignant, absolutely outraged. I've rarely seen anyone so incensed.

**BERENGER.** Well, for once I'm on his side. He's a good man after all. He's a very worthwhile person – and they're not easy to find these days. He's down-to-earth, with four feet planted firmly on the ground – I mean, both feet. I'm in complete agreement with him. I shall congratulate him when I see him. I deplore Mr. Papillon's action; it was his duty not to succumb.

**DUDARD.** How intolerant you are. Maybe Papillon felt the need for a bit of relaxation after all these years of office life.

>   *(He moves to the table, plucks the flower from the plant on it and eats the flower.)*

**BERENGER.** *(Sitting on the bed; ironically.)* And you're too tolerant, far too broadminded.

DUDARD. My dear Berenger, one must always make an effort to understand. And in order to understand a phenomenon and its effects you need to work back to the initial causes, by honest intellectual effort. We must try to do this – because, after all, we are thinking beings. I haven't yet succeeded, as I told you, and I don't know if I shall succeed. But at any rate one must start out favorably disposed – or at least impartial; one has to keep an open mind that's essential to a scientific mentality. Everything is logical. To understand is to justify.

BERENGER. You'll be siding with the rhinoceroses before long.

DUDARD. *(Moving left and picking his teeth.)* No, no, not at all. I wouldn't go that far. I'm simply trying to look the facts unemotionally in the face. I'm trying to be realistic. I also contend that there is no real evil in what occurs naturally.

> *(He moves above the table.)*

BERENGER. And you consider all this natural?

DUDARD. What could be more natural than a rhinoceros?

> *(He coughs in a hoarse voice and looks very surprised.)*

BERENGER. Yes, but for a man to turn into a rhinoceros is abnormal beyond question.

DUDARD. Well, of course, that's a matter of opinion.

BERENGER. It is beyond question, absolutely beyond question!

DUDARD. You seem very sure of yourself. Who can say where the normal stops and the abnormal begins? Can you personally define these conceptions of normality and abnormality? Nobody has solved this problem yet, either medically or philosophically. You ought to know that.

BERENGER. The problem may not be resolved philosophically –

*(He rises.)*

**BERENGER.** – but in practice it's simple. They may prove there's no such thing as movement – and then you start walking.

*(He circles the room.)*

And you go on walking, and you say to yourself, like Galileo, *"E pur si muove."*

**DUDARD.** You're getting things all mixed up. Don't confuse the issue. In Galileo's case it was the opposite: theoretic and scientific thought proving superior to mass opinion and dogmatism.

**BERENGER.** *(Moving to right of the table center; quite lost.)* What does all that mean? Mass opinion, dogmatism – they're just words. I may be mixing everything up in my head but you're losing yours. You don't know what's normal and what isn't any more. I couldn't care less about Galileo – I don't give a damn about Galileo.

*(He moves downstage right.)*

**DUDARD.** You brought him up in the first place and raised the whole question, saying that practice always had the last word. Maybe it does, but only when it proceeds from theory. The history of thought and science proves that.

*(He sits left of the table.)*

**BERENGER.** *(More and more furious.)* It doesn't prove anything of the sort.

*(He moves to right of the table center and beats on it.)*

It's all gibberish, utter lunacy!

**DUDARD.** There again, we need to define exactly what we mean by lunacy.

**BERENGER.** Lunacy is lunacy and that's all there is to it. Everybody knows what lunacy is. And what about the rhinoceroses – are they practice or are they theory?

**DUDARD**. Both.

**BERENGER**. How do you mean – both?

**DUDARD**. Both the one and the other, or one or the other. It's a debatable point.

**BERENGER**. Well, in that case –

*(He moves downstage right.)*

I refuse to think about it.

**DUDARD**. Now don't get so het up. Our opinions may not exactly coincide but we can still discuss the matter peaceably. These things should be discussed.

**BERENGER**. *(Distracted.)* You think I'm getting all het up, do you?

*(He gives a bellow like a rhinoceros and stands petrified for a few moments.)*

I might be Jean. Oh, no, no, I don't want to become like him. I mustn't be like him.

*(He calms down and moves to right of* **DUDARD**.*)*

I'm not very well up in philosophy. I've never studied; you've got all sorts of diplomas. That's why you're so at ease in discussion, whereas I never know what to answer – I'm so clumsy.

*(Rhinoceroses are heard passing under the window upstage left. He leans on the table.)*

*(Softly and very earnest.)* But I do feel you're in the wrong – I feel it instinctively – no, that's not what I mean, it's the rhinoceros which has instinct – I feel it intuitively, yes, that's the word – intuitively.

**DUDARD**. What do you understand by "intuitively"?

**BERENGER**. Intuitively means – well, just like that. I feel it, just like that. I think your excessive tolerance, and your generous indulgence – believe me, they're really only weakness – just blind spots...

*(Increase sound.)*

**DUDARD.** You're innocent enough to think that.

**BERENGER.** *(Pacing downstage right.)* You'll always be able to dance rings round me.

> *(He returns to right of the table.)*

But you know what? I'm going to try and get hold of the Logician.

**DUDARD.** What logician?

**BERENGER.** The Logician, the philosopher, a logician, you know – you know better than I do what a logician is. A logician I met, who explained to me...

**DUDARD.** What did he explain to you?

**BERENGER.** He explained that the Asiatic rhinoceroses were African and the African ones Asiatic.

**DUDARD.** I don't follow you.

**BERENGER.** No – no – he proved the contrary – that the African ones were Asiatic and the Asiatic ones – I know what I mean. That's not what I wanted to say. But you'll get on very well with him. He's your sort of person, a very good man, a very subtle mind, brilliant.

> *(Sound loud.)*

> *(There are increasing noises from the rhinoceroses. The words of the two men are drowned by the animals passing. For a few moments the lips of **DUDARD** and **BERENGER** are seen to move without any words being heard.)*

There they go again.

> *(He runs to the window upstage left.)*

Will they never stop! *(He shouts.)* Stop it! Stop it! You devils!

> *(He shakes his fist out of the window. The noises fade.)*

**DUDARD.** I'd be happy to meet your Logician. If he can enlighten me on these obscure and delicate points, I'd be only too delighted.

*(He takes a cigarette from his case but does not light it.)*

**BERENGER.** Yes, I'll bring him along, he'll talk to you. He's a very distinguished person, you'll see.

*(He shakes his fist out of the window.)*

You devils!

**DUDARD.** Let them alone. And be more polite. You shouldn't talk to people like that.

*(The sound of the rhinoceroses comes from the front of the stage.* **BERENGER** *runs to the imaginary window downstage center and looks out.)*

**BERENGER.** There they go again.

*(A boater pierced by a rhinoceros horn emerges from the orchestra pit under the imaginary window and passes with other rhinoceros cut-outs from right to left.)*

There's a boater impaled on a rhinoceros horn. Oh, it's the Logician's hat. It's the Logician's. That's the bloody limit! The Logician's turned into a rhinoceros.

**DUDARD.** *(Rising.)* That's no reason to be coarse.

*(He moves to left of* **BERENGER.***)*

**BERENGER.** Dear Lord, who can you turn to – who? I ask you. The Logician a rhinoceros.

*(He moves upstage right.)*

**DUDARD.** *(Looking out front.)* Where is he?

*(The cut-outs are illuminated by a green spotlight.* **BERENGER** *moves to right of* **DUDARD.***)*

**BERENGER.** *(Pointing.)* There, that one there, you see.

**DUDARD.** He's the only rhinoceros in a boater. That makes you think. You're sure it's your Logician?

**BERENGER.** The Logician – a rhinoceros!

**DUDARD**. He's still retained a vestige of his old individuality.

**BERENGER**. *(He shakes his fist at the cut-outs as they disappear and the spotlight fades.)* I'll never join up with you. Not me!

> *(He moves upstage right center.)*

**DUDARD**. If he was a genuine thinker, as you say, he couldn't have got carried away. He must have weighed all the pros and cons before deciding.

**BERENGER**. *(Shouting out front.)* I'll never join up with you.

**DUDARD**. Yes, that certainly makes you think.

> *(The rhinoceros sounds are heard outside the window upstage left.)*

**BERENGER**. *(Crossing to the window upstage left and shouting.)* No, I'll never join up with you.

**DUDARD**. They're going round and round the house. They're playing. Just big babies.

> *(He eats his cigarette. There is a knock on the door left.)*

There's somebody at the door, Berenger.

**BERENGER**. *(Shouting out of the window.)* It's a disgrace, masquerading like this – a disgrace!

**DUDARD**. *(Moving toward the door left.)* There's someone knocking, Berenger, can't you hear?

**BERENGER**. *(Crossing to right.)* Open, then, if you want to.

> *(**BERENGER** exits right **DUDARD** goes to the door left, and opens it. **DAISY** enters left. She carries a basket of food.)*

**DAISY**. Morning, Mr. Dudard.

**DUDARD**. Oh, it's you, Miss Daisy.

**DAISY**. Is Berenger here – is he any better?

**DUDARD**. How nice to see you, my dear. Do you often visit Berenger?

**DAISY**. Where is he?

> *(She moves left center.)*

**DUDARD**. *(Pointing right.)* In there.

> *(He closes the door.)*

**DAISY**. *(Moving above the table center.)* He's all on his own, poor thing. And he's not very well at the moment. Somebody has to give him a hand.

**DUDARD**. You're a good friend, Miss Daisy.

**DAISY**. That's just what I am – a good friend.

**DUDARD**. You've got a warm heart.

**DAISY**. I'm a good friend, that's all.

> (**BERENGER** *enters right, carrying a glass of water.* **DAISY** *puts the basket upstage center and meets* **BERENGER** *right center.)*

**BERENGER**. Oh, Miss Daisy. How kind of you to come, how very kind.

**DUDARD**. *(Moving left center.)* It certainly is.

**BERENGER**. *(Moving right.)* Did you know, Miss Daisy –

> *(He hides the brandy bottle under the pillow on the bed, then takes an aspirin tablet.)*

that the Logician is a rhinoceros?

**DAISY**. *(Moving downstage right center.)* Yes, I did. I caught sight of him in the street as I arrived. He was running very fast for someone his age. Are you feeling any better, Mr. Berenger?

**BERENGER**. My head's still bad. Still got a headache. Isn't it frightful?

> *(He moves to the clothes horse.)*

What do you think about it?

**DAISY**. *(Moving to* **BERENGER**.) I think you ought to be resting.

> (**BERENGER** *takes the clothes from the clothes horse and hands them to* **DAISY**.)

You should take things quietly for a few more days.

**DUDARD**. I hope I'm not disturbing you?

**BERENGER.** *(To* **DAISY.***)* I meant about the Logician.

*(He picks up the clothes horse and folds it.)*

**DAISY.** *(To* **DUDARD.***)* Why should you be? *(To* **BERENGER.***)* Oh, about the Logician. I don't think anything at all.

**DUDARD.** *(To* **DAISY.***)* I thought I might be in the way.

**DAISY.** *(To* **BERENGER.***)* What do you expect me to think? *(To both.)* I've got some news for you – Botard's a rhinoceros.

> **(BERENGER** *drops the clothes horse,* **DAISY** *cries out and drops the clothes.)*

**DUDARD.** Well, well!

**BERENGER.** *(Picking up the clothes horse.)* I don't believe it. He was against it. You must be mistaken.

> **(DAISY** *picks up the clothes and puts them on the table center.)*

He protested. Dudard has just been telling me. Isn't that so, Dudard?

**DUDARD.** That is so.

**DAISY.** *(Taking the clothes horse from* **BERENGER** *and putting it right.)* I know he was against it. But it didn't stop him turning, twenty-four hours after Mr. Papillon.

**DUDARD.** Well, he must have changed his mind. Everybody has the right to do that.

**BERENGER.** *(Crossing to left of the table; desperately.)* Then obviously anything can happen.

**DUDARD.** *(To* **BERENGER.***)* He was a very good man according to you just now.

**BERENGER.** *(To* **DAISY.***)* I just can't believe it. They must have lied to you.

**DAISY.** *(Moving above the table center.)* I saw him do it.

**BERENGER.** Then he must have been lying; he was just pretending.

**DAISY.** *(Folding the clothes on the table.)* He seemed very sincere; sincerity itself.

**BERENGER.** Did he give any reasons?

**DAISY.** What he said was, "We must move with the times." Those were his last human words.

**BERENGER.** "Move with the times."

*(He sits left of the table.)*

**DUDARD.** *(Crossing above* **BERENGER** *to left of* **DAISY**.*)* I was almost certain I'd meet you here, Miss Daisy.

**BERENGER.** *(To himself.)* What a mentality!

*(He makes a wide gesture.)*

**DUDARD.** *(Putting his hand on* **DAISY**'s *shoulder.)* Impossible to find you anywhere else, since the office closed.

**BERENGER.** *(Aside.)* What childishness.

*(He repeats the same gesture.)*

**DAISY.** *(To* **DUDARD**.*)* If you wanted to see me, you only had to telephone.

**DUDARD.** Oh, you know me, Miss Daisy – I'm discretion itself.

*(**DAISY** picks up the folded clothes, crosses, and puts them on the table right.)*

**BERENGER.** But now I come to think it over, Botard's behaviour doesn't surprise me.

*(**DUDARD** crosses to right center. **DAISY** goes upstage center and picks up her basket.)*

His firmness was only a pose. Which doesn't stop him from being a good man, of course. Good men make good rhinoceroses, unfortunately. It's because they are so good they get taken in.

**DAISY.** Do you mind if I put this basket on the table?

*(She puts the basket on the table right center.)*

**BERENGER.** But he was a good man with a lot of resentment.

**DUDARD.** *(To* **DAISY**; *hastening to help her with the basket.)* Excuse me, excuse us both, we should have given you a hand before.

**BERENGER**. He hated his superiors, and he'd got an inferiority complex.

**DUDARD**. (*Moving downstage right; expansively.*) Your argument doesn't hold water, because the example he followed was the chief's, the very instrument of the people who exploited him. As he used to say.

> (**DAISY** *transfers the plant from the table center to the chest of drawers upstage left. She does a "take" at the lack of a flower.*)

No, with him it was a case of community spirit triumphing over his anarchic impulses.

> (**DAISY** *gets a white cloth from the chest of drawers and moves to the table center.*)

**BERENGER**. It's the rhinoceroses which are anarchic, because they're in the minority.

**DUDARD**. They are, it's true – for the moment.

**DAISY**. (*Spreading the cloth.*) They're a pretty big minority, and getting bigger all the time.

> (**BERENGER** *rises and helps* **DAISY** *with the cloth.*)

My cousin's a rhinoceros now, and his wife. Not to mention leading personalities like the Cardinal of Retz.

**DUDARD**. A prelate!

**DAISY**. Mazarin.

**DUDARD**. This is going to spread to other countries, you'll see.

**BERENGER**. And to think it all started with us.

**DAISY**. And some of the aristicracy. The Duke of St. Simon.

**BERENGER**. (*Sitting left of the table; with uplifted arms.*) All our great names.

**DAISY**. And others, too. Lots of others. Maybe a quarter of the whole town.

**BERENGER**. We're still in the majority. We must take advantage of that. We must do something before we're inundated.

**DUDARD.** They're very potent, very.

**DAISY.** *(Unpacking her basket on to the table center.)* Well, for the moment, let's eat.

**BERENGER.** You've brought some food. You're very kind, Miss Daisy.

**DUDARD.** *(Aside.)* Very kind indeed.

**BERENGER.** I don't know how to thank you.

**DAISY.** *(To* **DUDARD.***)* Would you care to eat with us?

**DUDARD.** *(Moving downstage right center; uneasily.)* I don't want to be a nuisance.

**DAISY.** Whatever do you mean, Mr. Dudard? You know very well we'd love you to stay.

**DUDARD.** Well, you know. I'd hate to be in the way.

**BERENGER.** Of course, stay, Dudard. It's always a pleasure to talk to you.

**DUDARD.** *(Moving to right of the table.)* As a matter of fact I'm in a bit of a hurry. I have an appointment.

**BERENGER.** Just now you said you'd got nothing to do.

**DAISY.** You know, I had a lot of trouble finding food. The shops have been plundered; they just devour everything. And a lot of the shops are closed. It's written up outside: "Closed on account of transformation."

> *(She puts her empty basket on the floor upstage left.)*

**BERENGER.** They should be all rounded up in a big enclosure, and kept under strict supervision.

**DUDARD.** That's easier said than done. The animal's protection league would never allow it.

**DAISY.** And besides, everyone has a close relative or a friend among them, and that would make it even more difficult.

**BERENGER.** So everybody's mixed up in it.

> *(***DAISY*** exits right.)*

**DUDARD.** Everybody's in the same boat.

**BERENGER**. But how can people be rhinoceroses? It doesn't bear thinking about.

> *(He rises, moves center and calls to* **DAISY**.*)*

Shall I help you lay the table?

**DAISY**. *(Offstage.)* No, don't bother. I know where the plates are.

**DUDARD**. *(Aside.)* She's obviously very familiar with the place.

**DAISY**. *(She enters right with three plates, knives and forks. To* **DUDARD**.*)* I'm laying for three – all right? You are staying with us?

> *(She sets the plates etc. on the table.)*

**BERENGER**. Yes, of course he's staying.

**DAISY**. *(To* **BERENGER**.*)* You get used to it, you know. Nobody seems surprised any more to see herds of rhinoceroses galloping through the streets. They just stand aside, and then carry on as if nothing had happened.

**DUDARD**. It's the wisest course to take.

**BERENGER**. Well, I can't get used to it.

**DUDARD**. *(Reflectively.)* I wonder if one oughtn't to give it a try.

**DAISY**. Well, right now, let's have lunch.

**BERENGER**. I don't see how a legal man like yourself can.

> *(Cue No. 10: A great noise of rhinoceroses traveling very fast is heard outside. Trumpets and drums are also heard.)*

What's going on?

> *(***BERENGER*** *and* ***DUDARD*** *rush to the imaginary window downstage center.)*

What is it?

> *(Cue B: The sound of a wall crumbling is heard.)*

You can't see a thing. What's happening?

**DUDARD**. You can't see, but you can hear all right.

**BERENGER**. That's no good.

**DAISY**. *(Fussing over the table.)* The plates will be all covered in dust.

**BERENGER**. How unhygienic!

**DAISY**. Let's hurry up and eat. We won't pay any attention to them.

**BERENGER**. *(Pointing out front.)* They've demolished the walls of the fire station.

**DUDARD**. That's true, they've demolished them.

**DAISY**. *(She joins the other two downstage center.)* They're coming out.

**BERENGER**. All the firemen, a whole regiment of rhinoceroses, led by drums.

**DAISY**. They're pouring up the streets.

**BERENGER**. It's gone too far, much too far.

**DAISY**. More rhinoceroses are streaming out of the courtyard.

**BERENGER**. And out of the houses.

**DUDARD**. And the windows as well.

**DAISY**. They're joining up with the others.

**DUDARD**. There aren't enough of us left any more.

> *(Sound out.)*

**BERENGER**. How many with one horn, and how many with two?

**DUDARD**. The statisticians are bound to be compiling statistics now. There'll be plenty of erudite controversy, you can be sure.

**BERENGER**. They can only calculate approximately. It's all happening so fast. It leaves them no time. No time to calculate.

**DAISY**. The best thing is to let the statisticians get on with it.

> *(She leads **BERENGER** to left of the table.)*

Come and eat, my dear.

*(*BERENGER *sits docilely left of the table.)*

That'll calm you down. You'll feel better afterwards. *(To* **DUDARD**.*)* And you, too.

**DUDARD**. *(Moving downstage right.)* I don't feel very hungry –

*(He moves upstage right center and points to the table.)*

or rather, to be frank, I don't like tinned food very much. I feel like eating outside on the grass.

**BERENGER**. *(Rising apprehensively.)* You mustn't do that. Think of the risk.

**DUDARD**. But really, I don't want to put you to the trouble.

**BERENGER**. But we've already told you –

**DUDARD**. *(Interrupting.)* I really mean it.

**DAISY**. *(Crossing to* **DUDARD**.*)* Of course, if you really don't want to stay, we can't force you.

**DUDARD**. I didn't mean to offend you.

**BERENGER**. Don't let him go, he mustn't go.

**DAISY**. *(Crossing to right of* **DUDARD**.*)* I'd like him to stay –

*(*DUDARD *moves restlessly right center.)*

but people must do as they please.

**BERENGER**. *(Moving to left of* **DUDARD**.*)* Man is superior to the rhinoceros.

**DUDARD**. *(Looking out of the imaginary window downstage center.)* I didn't say he wasn't.

*(He turns away upstage right center.)*

But I'm not with you absolutely, either.

*(He returns to the imaginary window.)*

I don't know; only experience can tell.

**BERENGER**. *(Moving to left of* **DUDARD**.*)* You're weakening, too, Dudard. It's just a passing phase which you'll regret.

**DAISY**. If it's just a passing phase then there's no great danger.

**DUDARD.** I feel certain scruples. I feel it's my duty to stick by my employers and my friends, through thick and thin.

**BERENGER.** It's not as if you were married to them.

**DUDARD.** I've renounced marriage. I prefer the great universal family to the little domestic one.

**DAISY.** *(Softly.)* We shall miss you a lot, Dudard, but we can't do anything about it.

**DUDARD.** It's my duty to stick by them; I have to do my duty.

> *(***DAISY*** crosses to left center.)*

**BERENGER.** *(Restraining* **DUDARD.***)* No, you're wrong, your duty is to – you don't see where your real duty lies – your duty is to oppose them, with a firm, clear mind.

**DUDARD.** I shall keep my mind clear.

> *(He breaks from* **BERENGER** *and runs upstage left center.* **BERENGER** *moves to right of the table.* **DAISY,** *alarmed, moves to the door left.)*

As clear as ever it was. But if you're going to criticize, it's better to do so from the inside. I'm not going to abandon them.

> *(He runs downstage right, jumps on to the bed, and crumples the bedclothes.)*

I won't abandon them.

> *(***DUDARD,*** *with his back to the audience, fixes a small horn to his forehead, the horn having been previously pre-set in the bed.)*

**DAISY.** He's very good-hearted.

> *(Cue No. 11.)*

**BERENGER.** He's too good-hearted. *(To* **DUDARD.***)* You're too good-hearted, you're human. *(To* **DAISY.***)* Don't let him go. He's making a mistake. He's human.

> *(***DUDARD** *leaps from the bed, showing the horn, and charges toward the door left.)*

**DAISY.** What can I do?

*(She opens the door and flattens herself against the wall.)*

*(***DUDARD*** charges out left. ***DAISY*** goes to the window upstage left.)*

**BERENGER.** *(Running to the door left and calling.)* Come back, Dudard! We're fond of you, don't go.

*(He slams the door.)*

It's too late. Too late!

**DAISY.** We couldn't do anything.

*(The sound of the rhinoceroses is heard outside the window upstage left. ***BERENGER*** moves to the window up left.)*

**BERENGER.** He's joined up with them. Where is he now?

**DAISY.** *(Looking out of the window.)* With them.

**BERENGER.** Which one is he?

**DAISY.** You can't tell. You can't recognize him anymore.

**BERENGER.** They all look alike, all alike. You should have held him back by force.

*(He moves below the table.)*

**DAISY.** I didn't dare to.

**BERENGER.** *(Moving downstage right.)* You should have been firmer with him; you should have insisted; he was in love with you, wasn't he?

**DAISY.** He never made me any official declaration.

**BERENGER.** *(Moving right center.)* Everybody knew he was. He's done this out of thwarted love. He was a shy man. He wanted to make a big gesture to impress you. Don't you feel like going after him?

**DAISY.** Not at all. Or I wouldn't be here.

**BERENGER.** *(Looking out of the imaginary window.)* You can see nothing but them in the street. Nothing but them. You were wrong, Daisy.

*(***DAISY*** crosses to the bed and tidies the covers.)*

**BERENGER**. Not a single human being as far as the eye can see. They're all over the street. Half with one horn and half with two, and that's the only distinction.

> *(Sound louder.)*

> *(Powerful noises of moving rhinoceroses are heard, but somehow it is a musical sound. He moves tentatively to the left of* **DAISY**.*)*

You don't feel let down, do you, Daisy? There's nothing you regret?

**DAISY**. No, no.

> *(She continues with the bed.)*

**BERENGER**. I want so much to be a comfort to you.

> *(He puts a hand on her back.* **DAISY** *turns to him.)*

I love you, Daisy; don't ever leave me.

**DAISY**. *(After a pause.)* Shut the window, darling.

> *(***BERENGER** *crosses and shuts the window upstage left.)*

> *(Fade out Cue No. 11.)*

They're making such a noise.

> *(She finishes the bed making.)*

And the dust is rising even up to here. Everything will get filthy.

**BERENGER**. I'm not afraid of anything as long as we're together.

> *(He crosses to* **DAISY**. *She sits on the bed.)*

I don't care what happens. You know, Daisy, I thought I'd never be able to fall in love again.

> *(He takes her hand and squats in front of her.)*

**DAISY**. Well, you see, everything is possible.

**BERENGER**. I want so much to make you happy. Do you think you can be happy with me?

**DAISY**. Why not? If you're happy, then I'll be happy, too. You say nothing scares you, but you're really frightened of everything. What can possibly happen to us?

**BERENGER**. *(Stammering.)* My love, my dear love.

*(He rises.)*

Let me kiss your lips.

*(He kisses her, springs away from her, then returns and holds her hands.)*

I never dreamed I could still feel such tremendous emotion.

**DAISY**. You must be more calm and more sure of yourself, now.

**BERENGER**. I am. Let me kiss you again.

*(He kisses her.)*

**DAISY**. Come and sit down.

*(**BERENGER** sits above **DAISY** on the bed, puts his feet up and his head in her lap.)*

**BERENGER**. There was no point in Dudard quarreling with Botard, as things turned out.

**DAISY**. Don't think about Dudard any more. I'm here with you. We've no right to interfere in other people's lives.

**BERENGER**. But you're interfering in mine. You know how to be firm with me.

**DAISY**. That's not the same thing; I never loved Dudard.

**BERENGER**. I see what you mean. If he'd stayed he'd always have been an obstacle between us. Ah, happiness is such an egotistical thing!

**DAISY**. You have to fight for happiness, don't you agree?

**BERENGER**. I adore you, Daisy; I admire you as well.

**DAISY**. Maybe you won't say that when you get to know me better.

**BERENGER**. The more I know you the better you seem; and you're so beautiful, so very beautiful.

*(Cue No. 11, continued: More rhinoceroses are heard passing.)*

**BERENGER**. Particularly compared to them.

> *(He points to the window.)*

You probably think that's no compliment, but they make you seem more beautiful than ever.

**DAISY**. Have you been good today? You haven't had any brandy?

**BERENGER**. Oh, yes, I've been good.

**DAISY**. Is that the truth?

**BERENGER**. Yes, it's the truth, I assure you.

**DAISY**. Can I believe you, I wonder?

**BERENGER**. *(A little flustered.)* Oh, yes, you must believe me.

> *(He sits up and swings his legs off the bed, embarrassed.)*

**DAISY**. Well, all right, then, you can have a little glass. It'll buck you up.

> *(**BERENGER** is about to leap up.)*

You stay where you are, dear. Where's the bottle?

> *(She rises and crosses to center.)*

**BERENGER**. *(He takes the bottle from under the pillow.)* Here.

**DAISY**. *(Moving to **BERENGER**.)* You've hidden it well away.

> *(She sits below **BERENGER** on the bed, takes the bottle from him and pours a drink.)*

**BERENGER**. It's out of the way of temptation.

**DAISY**. You've been a good boy. You're making progress.

> *(**BERENGER** rises, then sits on the floor at **DAISY**'s feet and rest his head on her lap.)*

**BERENGER**. I'll make a lot more now I'm with you.

**DAISY**. *(Handing the drink to him.)* Here you are. That's your reward.

**BERENGER**. Thank you.

> *(He downs the drink at one go and holds out his empty glass.)*

**DAISY.** Oh, no, dear. That's enough for this morning.

> *(She takes the glass and puts it with the bottle on the table right center.)*

I don't want it to make you ill. How's your head feel now?

**BERENGER.** Much better, darling.

**DAISY.** Then we'll take off the bandage. It doesn't suit you at all.

**BERENGER.** Oh, no, don't touch it.

**DAISY.** Nonsense, we'll take it off now.

**BERENGER.** I'm frightened there might be something underneath.

**DAISY.** *(Removing the bandage.)* Always frightened, aren't you, always imagining the worst.

> *(She throws the bandage on to the upstage end of the bed.)*

There's nothing there, you see. Your forehead's as smooth as a baby's.

**BERENGER.** *(Feeling his brow.)* You're right; you're getting rid of my complexes.

> *(**DAISY** kisses him on the brow.)*

What should I do without you?

**DAISY.** I'll never leave you alone again.

**BERENGER.** I won't have any more fears now I'm with you.

**DAISY.** I'll keep them all at bay.

**BERENGER.** We'll read books together. I'll become clever.

**DAISY.** And when there aren't so many people about we'll go for long walks.

**BERENGER.** Yes, along the Seine, and in the Luxembourg Gardens.

**DAISY.** And to the zoo.

**BERENGER.** I'll be brave and strong. I'll keep you safe from harm.

**DAISY**. You won't need to defend me, silly. We don't wish anyone any harm. And no one wishes us any, my dear.

**BERENGER**. Sometimes one does harm without meaning to, or rather one allows it to go unchecked. I shall never forgive myself for not being nicer to Jean. I never managed to give him a really solid proof of the friendship I felt for him. I wasn't sufficiently understanding with him.

**DAISY**. Don't worry about it. You did all you could. There's no point in reproaching yourself now. You must forget all those bad memories.

**BERENGER**. But they keep coming back to me. They're very real memories.

**DAISY**. I never knew you were such a realist – I thought you were more poetic. Where's your imagination? There are many sides to reality. Choose the one that's best for you. Escape into the world of the imagination.

**BERENGER**. It's easy to say that.

**DAISY**. Aren't I enough for you?

**BERENGER**. Oh yes, more than enough.

**DAISY**. You'll spoil everything if you go on having a bad conscience. Everybody has their faults, but you and I have got less than a lot of people.

**BERENGER**. Do you really think so?

**DAISY**. We're comparatively better than most. We're good, both of us.

**BERENGER**. That's true, you're good and I'm good. That's true.

**DAISY**. Well then, we have the right to live. We even owe ourselves a duty to be happy in spite of everything. Guilt is a dangerous symptom. It shows a lack of purity.

**BERENGER**. You're right, it can lead to that –

*(He points to the window upstage left.)*

*(Cue No. 11, continued: More rhinoceroses are heard passing.)*

– a lot of them started like that.

**DAISY.** We must try and not feel guilty anymore.

**BERENGER.** How right you are, my wonderful love. You're all my happiness; the light of my life. We are together, aren't we? No one can separate us. Our love is the only thing that's real. Nobody has the right to stop us from being happy – in fact, nobody could, could they?

*(The telephone rings.)*

Who could that be?

**DAISY.** *(Fearful.)* Don't answer.

**BERENGER.** Why not?

**DAISY.** I don't know. I just feel it's better not to.

**BERENGER.** It might be Mr. Papillon, or Botard, or Jean or Dudard ringing to say they've had second thoughts. You did say it was probably only a passing phase.

**DAISY.** I don't think so. They wouldn't have changed their minds so quickly. They've not had time to think it over. They're bound to give it a fair trial.

**BERENGER.** Perhaps the authorities have decided to take action at last; maybe they're ringing to ask our help.

**DAISY.** I'd be surprised if it was them.

*(The telephone rings. They rise.)*

**BERENGER.** *(Moving downstage right.)* It is the authorities, I tell you, I recognize the ring – a long, drawn-out ring. I can't ignore an appeal from them. It can't be anyone else.

*(He lifts the receiver. Into the telephone.)*

Hallo? ...

*(Cue C: Trumpetings are heard coming from the receiver.)*

You hear that? Trumpeting! Listen!

*(Three rhino calls.)*

*(**DAISY** takes the receiver, listens a moment, is shocked by the sound, quickly replaces the receiver and backs center.)*

**DAISY**. *(Frightened.)* What's going on?

**BERENGER**. They're playing jokes now.

**DAISY**. Jokes in bad taste.

**BERENGER**. You see! What did I tell you?

**DAISY**. You didn't tell me anything.

**BERENGER**. I was expecting that; it was just what I'd predicted.

**DAISY**. You didn't predict anything. You never do. You can only predict things after they've happened.

**BERENGER**. Oh, yes, I can; I can predict things, all right.

**DAISY**. *(Crossing above the table to left of it.)* That's not nice of them – in fact it's very nasty. I don't like being made fun of.

**BERENGER**. *(Moving center.)* They wouldn't dare make fun of you. It's me they're making fun of.

**DAISY**. And naturally I come in for it as well because I'm with you. They're taking their revenge. But what have we done to them?

> *(Cue C: The telephone rings.)*

Pull the plug out.

**BERENGER**. *(Moving to right of* **DAISY**.*)* The telephone authorities say you mustn't.

**DAISY**. Oh, you never dare to do anything – and you say you could defend me.

**BERENGER**. *(Darting to the radio.)* Let's turn on the radio for the news.

> *(He switches on the radio.)*

**DAISY**. *(Following* **BERENGER**.*)* Yes, we must find out how things stand.

> *(Cue C: The sound of trumpeting comes from the radio.)*

> *(**BERENGER** peremptorily switches it off, but in the distance other trumpetings, like echoes, can be heard. She recoils in terror.)*

What's happening?

**BERENGER.** *(Very agitated.)* What are they doing? Keep calm. Keep calm!

**DAISY.** They've taken over the radio stations.

**BERENGER.** *(Moving downstage left center; agitated and trembling.)* Keep calm, keep calm.

**DAISY.** *(Moving to the imaginary window.)* It's no joke any longer. They mean business.

**BERENGER.** *(Moving to left of* **DAISY.***)* There's only them left now; nobody but them. Even the authorities have joined them.

> *(There is a pause. They stand looking out front, very still and quiet.)*

**DAISY.** Not a soul left anywhere.

**BERENGER.** *(After a pause.)* We're all alone, we're left all alone.

**DAISY.** That's what you wanted.

**BERENGER.** You mean that's what you wanted.

**DAISY.** It was you.

**BERENGER.** You!

> *(Cue D: Noises come from everywhere at once. From left and right in the house, the noise of rushing feet and the panting breath of the animals.)*

> *(But all these disquieting sounds are nevertheless somehow rhythmical, making a kind of music. The loudest noises of all come from above; a noise of stamping. Plaster falls from the ceiling. The house shakes violently.)*

**DAISY.** The earth's trembling.

> *(She does not know where to run.)*

**BERENGER.** *(Moving to the door left and opening it.)* No, that's our neighbours, the Perissodactyls. *(He shouts.)* Stop it! You're preventing us from working. Noise is forbidden in these flats. Noise is forbidden.

DAISY. *(Leaning on the downstage right corner of the table.)* They'll never listen to you.

> *(However the noise does diminish, merely forming a sort of musical background.)*

BERENGER. *(Afraid.)* Don't be frightened, my dear.

> *(He runs to DAISY and puts his arms around her.)*

We're together. You're happy with me, aren't you? I'll chase all your fears away.

DAISY. Perhaps it's all our own fault.

BERENGER. Don't think about it any longer. We mustn't start feeling remorse. It's dangerous to start feeling guilty.

> *(Fade out sound.)*

We must just live our lives, and be happy. We have the right to be happy. They're not spiteful, and we're not doing them any harm. They'll leave us in peace. You just keep calm and rest. Sit down.

> *(He leads DAISY to the bed.)*

Just keep calm.

> *(DAISY sits on the bed. He kneels beside her.)*

Would you like a drop of brandy to pull you together?

DAISY. I've got a headache.

BERENGER. *(He rises, picks up his bandage and binds DAISY's head.)* I love you, my darling. Don't you worry, they'll get over it. It's just a passing phase.

DAISY. They won't get over it. It's for good.

BERENGER. I love you. I love you madly.

DAISY. *(Taking off the bandage.)* Let things just take their course. What can we do about it?

BERENGER. *(Sitting above DAISY on the bed.)* They've all gone mad. The world is sick. They're all sick.

DAISY. We shan't be the ones to cure them.

BERENGER. How can we live in the same house with them?

DAISY. *(Calming down.)* We must be sensible. We must adapt ourselves and try and get on with them.

BERENGER. They can't understand us.

DAISY. They must. There's no other way.

BERENGER. Do you understand them?

DAISY. Not yet. But we must try to understand the way their minds work, and learn their language.

> *(Cue No. 11, continued and as needed to the end of the play: The rhinoceroses are heard singing and grunting.)*

BERENGER. They haven't got a language. Listen – do you call that a language?

DAISY. How do you know? You're no polyglot.

BERENGER. We'll talk about it later.

> *(He rises and moves to the table.)*

We must have lunch first.

DAISY. I'm not hungry anymore. It's all too much. I can't take any more.

BERENGER. *(Moving to her; worried.)* But you're the strong one. You're not going to let it get you down. It's precisely for your courage that I admire you so.

DAISY. You said that before.

BERENGER. *(Squatting in front of her.)* Do you feel sure of my love?

DAISY. Yes, of course.

BERENGER. I love you so.

DAISY. You keep saying the same thing, my dear.

BERENGER. Listen, Daisy, there *is* something we can do. We'll have children, and our children will have children – it'll take time, but together we can regenerate the human race.

DAISY. Regenerate the human race?

BERENGER. It happened once before.

DAISY. Ages ago. Adam and Eve. They had a lot of courage.

**BERENGER.** And we, too, can have courage. We don't need all that much. It happens automatically with time and patience.

**DAISY.** What's the use?

**BERENGER.** Of course we can – with a little bit of courage.

**DAISY.** *(Rising and crossing to left.)* I don't want to have children – it's a bore.

**BERENGER.** *(Crossing to her.)* How can we save the world, if you don't?

**DAISY.** Why bother to save it?

**BERENGER.** *(Grabbing her by the shoulders.)* What a thing to say! Do it for me, Daisy. Let's save the world.

> *(On the upstage wall stylized rhinoceros heads appear and disappear; they become more and more numerous from now on until the end of the play. Toward the end they stay fixed for longer and longer, until eventually they fill the entire back wall, remaining static. The heads, in spite of their monstrous appearance, seem to become more and more beautiful.)*

**DAISY.** After all, perhaps it's we who need saving. Perhaps we're the abnormal ones.

**BERENGER.** You're not yourself, Daisy, you've got a touch of fever.

**DAISY.** There aren't any more of our kind about anywhere, are there?

**BERENGER.** *(Moving center.)* Daisy, you're not to talk like that.

**DAISY.** *(She looks all around at the rhinoceros heads on the wall at the back.)* Those are the real people. They look happy. They're content to be what they are. They were right to do what they did.

**BERENGER.** *(Clasping his hands and looking despairingly at* **DAISY**.*)* We're the ones who are doing right, Daisy, I assure you.

**DAISY**. That's very presumptuous of you.

**BERENGER**. You know perfectly well I'm right.

**DAISY**. There's no such thing as absolute right. It's the world that's right – not you and me.

**BERENGER**. I *am* right, Daisy. And the proof is that you understand me when I speak to you.

**DAISY**. What does that prove?

**BERENGER**. The proof is that I love you as much as it's possible for a man to love a woman.

**DAISY**. Funny sort of argument!

**BERENGER**. I don't understand you any longer, Daisy. You don't know what you're saying, darling. Think of our love.

> (*He moves to* **DAISY** *and holds her. Pleading and very earnest.*)

Our love...

**DAISY**. I feel a bit ashamed of what you call love – this morbid feeling, this male weakness. And female, too. It just doesn't compare with the ardour and the tremendous energy emanating from all these creatures around us.

**BERENGER**. Energy! You want some energy, do you? I can let you have some energy!

> (*He slaps her face.*)

**DAISY**. (*Turning away and leaning on the table.*) Oh! I never would have believed it possible.

**BERENGER**. (*Clasping her to him.*) Oh, forgive me, my darling, please forgive me. Forgive me, my darling. I didn't mean it. I don't know what came over me, losing control like that.

**DAISY**. (*Breaking from him and facing upstage.*) It's because you've run out of arguments, that's why.

**BERENGER**. (*Crossing slowly to right.*) Oh, dear! In the space of a few minutes we've gone through twenty-five years of married life.

**DAISY**. I pity you. I understand you all too well.

**BERENGER**. *(Turning away and speaking almost to himself.)* You're probably right that I've run out of arguments.

*(**DAISY** pulls herself together.)*

You think they're stronger than me, stronger than us. Maybe they are.

**DAISY**. Indeed they are.

**BERENGER**. Well, in spite of everything, I swear to you I'll never give in, never!

*(There is a pause during which **DAISY** moves slowly to **BERENGER** and puts her arms around his neck. They cling together.)*

**DAISY**. My poor darling, I'll help you to resist – to the very end.

**BERENGER**. Will you be capable of it?

**DAISY**. I give you my word. You can trust me.

*(The rhinoceros noises become melodious.)*

Listen, they're singing.

**BERENGER**. They're not singing, they're roaring.

**DAISY**. They're singing.

**BERENGER**. They're roaring, I tell you.

*(**DAISY** leads **BERENGER** to the imaginary window, still holding his arm.)*

**DAISY**. You're mad, they're singing.

**BERENGER**. You can't have a very musical ear, then.

**DAISY**. You don't know the first thing about music. Poor dear –

*(She looks out front.)*

and look, they're playing as well, and dancing.

**BERENGER**. You call that dancing?

**DAISY**. It's their way of dancing. They're beautiful.

**BERENGER**. They're disgusting!

**DAISY.** *(Turning and moving to the window upstage left.)* You're not to say unpleasant things about them. It upsets me.

> *(She looks out of the window.)*

**BERENGER.** I'm sorry.

> *(He follows* **DAISY**.*)*

I'm not going to quarrel on their account.

**DAISY.** They're like gods.

**BERENGER.** *(Turning away left center.)* You go too far, Daisy; take a good look at them.

**DAISY.** You mustn't be jealous, my dear.

**BERENGER.** I can see our opinions are directly opposed. It's better not to discuss the matter.

**DAISY.** *(Moving to* **BERENGER**.*)* Now, you mustn't be nasty.

> *(***DAISY** *tries to embrace* **BERENGER**, *who frees himself.)*

**BERENGER.** Then don't you be stupid.

> *(He breaks violently from her and crosses downstage right, where he looks closely at himself in the imaginary mirror.)*

**DAISY.** It's no longer possible for us to live together.

> *(She goes quietly to the door left* **BERENGER** *continues to examine himself in the mirror.)*

*(To herself.)* He isn't very nice, really, he isn't very nice.

> *(***DAISY** *exits slowly left the rhinoceros noises fade.)*

**BERENGER.** *(Still looking at himself in the mirror.)* Men aren't so bad looking, you know. And I'm not a particularly handsome specimen. Believe me, Daisy.

> *(He turns.)*

Daisy! Daisy!

> *(He moves and looks off right.)*

Where are you, Daisy? You can't do that to me.

*(He darts to the door left and calls.)*

Daisy! Daisy! Come back! Come back, my dear. You haven't even had your lunch. Daisy, don't leave me alone. Remember your promise. Daisy! Daisy!

*(He makes a despairing gesture and crosses to center.)*

Well, it was obvious we weren't getting along together. The home was broken up. It just wasn't working out. But she shouldn't have left like that with no explanation.

*(He looks all around.)*

She didn't even leave a message. That's no way to behave. *(He pauses.)* Now I'm all on my own.

*(He bundles everything off the table center on to the floor.)*

*(Angrily.)* But they won't get me.

*(He carefully closes the windows.)*

You won't get me.

*(He moves the table center and wedges it against the door left. He addresses all the rhinoceroses:)*

I'm not joining you; I don't understand you.

*(He piles two chairs against the table.)*

I'm staying as I am. I'm a human being. A human being.

*(He sits in the remaining chair.)*

It's an impossible situation. It's my fault she's gone. I meant everything to her. What'll become of her? That's one more person on my conscience. Poor little thing left all alone in this world of monsters. Nobody can help me find her, nobody, because there's nobody left.

*(There are fresh trumpetings and sounds of hectic racings off.)*

I can't bear the sound of them any longer.

*(He rises, moves to the chest of drawers and takes out some cotton wool.)*

I'm going to put cotton wool in my ears.

*(He moves downstage center, putting the wool in his ears.)*

The only solution is to convince them – but convince them of what? Can they be changed back? Can they? It would be a labour of Hercules, far beyond me. In any case, to convince them you'd have to talk to them. And to talk to them I'd have to learn their language. Or they'd have to learn mine.

*(He looks in the imaginary mirror.)*

But what language do I speak? What is my language? Am I talking French? Yes, it must be French. But what is French? I can call it French if I want, and nobody can say it isn't – I'm the only one who speaks it. *(He pauses.)* What am I saying? Do I understand what I'm saying? Do I? And what if it's true what Daisy said, and they're the ones in the right? A man's not ugly to look at, not ugly at all.

*(He examines himself, passing his hand over his face.)*

What a funny looking thing. What do I look like? What?

*(He runs to the chest of drawers, takes out a box of photographs, spills them on to the floor and kneels beside them.)*

Photographs!

*(He examines the photographs.)*

Who are all these people? Is it Mr. Papillon – or is it Daisy? And is that Botard or Dudard or Jean? Or is it me?

*(He holds up a photograph in each hand.)*

Now I recognize me: that's me, that's me. That's me that's me. I'm not good looking. I'm not good looking.

*(He drops the photographs.)*

They're the good looking ones. I was wrong. Oh, how I wish I was like them.

*(He rises and moves to the imaginary mirror.)*

I haven't got any horns, more's the pity. A smooth brow looks so ugly. I need one or two horns to give my sagging face a lift. Perhaps one will grow and I needn't be ashamed anymore – then I could go and join them. But it will never grow.

*(He looks at the palms of his hands.)*

My hands are so smooth. Oh, why won't they get rough?

*(He undoes his shirt to look at his chest in the mirror.)*

My skin is so slack. I can't stand this white, hairy body.

*(Trumpetings are heard.)*

Oh, I'd love to have a hard skin in that wonderful dull green color – a skin that looks decent naked without any hair on it, like theirs.

*(He listens to the trumpetings.)*

Their song is charming – a bit raucous, perhaps, but it does have charm.

*(He moves downstage right.)*

I wish I could do it. *(He tries to imitate them.)* Ahh, ahh, brr! No, that's not it. Try again, louder. Ahh, ahh, brr! No, that's not it, it's too feeble, it's got no drive behind it. I'm not trumpeting at all; I'm just howling. Ahh, ahh, brr!

*(He moves upstage center.)*

There's a big difference between howling and trumpeting. I've only myself to blame; I should have gone with them while there was still time. Now, it's too late.

*(He sees the heads on the back wall and backs from them downstage center, in horror.)*

Now I'm a monster, just a monster. Now I'll never become a rhinoceros, never, never. I've gone past changing.

*(He puts his hands to his face and turns to the imaginary mirror.)*

I want to, I really do, but I can't. I just can't. I can't stand the sight of me. I'm too ashamed.

*(He moves upstage center, sobbing, and falls on his face, his shoulders heaving.)*

I'm so ugly. People who try to hang on to their individuality always come to a bad end.

*(He pauses, then suddenly snaps out of it, rises, moves downstage right, grabs the bottle of brandy and a glass and sits on the chair center.)*

Oh, well, too bad. I'll take on all of them. I'll put up a fight against the lot of them, the whole lot of them. I'm the last man left, and I'm staying that way until the end. I'm not capitulating.

*(**BERENGER** drinks as a huge cut-out rhinoceros drops in from the flies and:)*

*(Curtain.)*

## FURNITURE AND PROPERTY LIST

ACT I

Scene One

*On stage:*

Table (left center). *On it:* cloth
Table (right center). *On it:* cloth
4 upright chairs. *On chair left of table right center*: ashtray
In *café* right: small table
*Above café entrance:* small table. *On it:* potted plant
*Below café entrance:* small table. *On it:* potted plant. *Against it:* menu
    board
Tree (left)
Pissoir with bucket (center)

*Offstage:*

Cat (Housewife)
Shopping basket. *In it:* provisions, carrots, celery (Housewife)
Broom (Grocer's Wife)
Dead cat (Housewife)
Bottle of wine (Grocer)
Tray. *On it:* 2 cognacs (Waitress)
Tray. *On it:* glasses (Waitress)
Glass of brandy (Waitress)
Box for dead cat (Housewife)
Large brandy (Proprietor)

*Personal:*

Jean: hat, gloves, cane, wrist-watch, nail file, comb, mirror, tie,
    handkerchief
Logician: eyeglass, straw hat, card
Old Gentleman: ivory-handled cane, paper, pencil
Berenger: handkerchief
Housewife: 100-franc note

*On stage:*

Shelves (right). *On them:* reference books, documents, clips of papers,
    proofs, Botard's protective sleeves, Berenger's protective sleeves
Table (right). *On it:* 2 desk lamps, proofs, inkstand, pens, ashtray,
    pencils, pencil sharpener
3 stools
2 waste-paper baskets
Filing cabinet. *In it:* 2 sets galley proofs, papers in clip, documents.
    *On it:* files with papers

Table (center). *On it:* time sheet, pencil, ashtray, diary, 2 upright chairs
Table (left). *On it:* covered typewriter, typing paper
Hat-stand. *On it:* Botard's overall, Berenger's overall
Rail for trap stairs
2 wall-brackets
Light fittings off
Windows closed
Shutters closed

*Offstage:*

Documents, notebook, pencil, pencil sharpener (Daisy)
Newspaper (Dudard)
Letter (Papillon)
Glass of water (Daisy)
Telephone (Daisy)
Ladder (Fireman)

*Personal:*

Daisy: handbag. *In it:* compact
Botard: Basque beret, spectacles, pencil
Dudard: spectacles, protective sleeve, cigarettes, lighter
Papillon: Legion of Honour rosette
Berenger: cap, gloves, stick, flower
Mrs. Bœuf: handbag. *In it:* telegram

*On stage:*

Chest of drawers. *On it:* runner, tray, 2 bottles, telephone, First Aid box
*In drawer:* shirts, ties, vests
Bed. *On it:* bedding
Armchair. *On it:* box with chest expander
Small table. *On it:* books, magazine with rice paper in back
Upright chair
Carpet on floor
Window curtains
Pictures on walls
*On floor up center:* plush tablecloth
*Under bed:* Jean's socks and shoes
Chandelier
Light switch left
Trick panel in back wall
Doors closed
Window closed
Window curtains closed
Chandelier off

*Offstage:*
  Green make-up (Jean)
  Small putty horn (Jean)
  Large putty horn (Jean)
  2 towels (Jean)
  Loofah (Jean)
  Rhinoceros horn for door (Jean)
  4 rhinoceros heads

*Personal:*
  Berenger: cap, stick, gloves

*On stage:*
  Table (right). *On it:* ornaments, books
  Bed. *On it:* bedding
  Small table. *On it:* table-lamp, telephone, tumbler, aspirins
  *On floor beside bed:* bottle of brandy
  Chest of drawers. *On it:* radio, plant with edible rose, duster
          *In it:* white cloth, box of photographs, cotton wool
  3 sets curtains
  3 upright chairs
  Cabinet (left)
  Heavy dining-table against door left
  Clothes line. *On it:* shirts, etc.
  Clothes horse. *On it:* clothes
  Carpet on floor
  Pictures on walls
  *In bed:* small horn
Window open
Doors closed
Window and door curtains closed
Lamp off

*Offstage:*
  Rhinoceros cut-outs
  Rhinoceros cut-out with boater
  Basket *In it:* loaf, 2 tins sardines, apples, melon, butter, cheese,
    sausage wine (Daisy)
  Glass of water (Berenger)
  3 plates, 3 knives, 3 forks (Daisy)

*Personal:*
  Berenger: bandage
  Dudard: edible cigarette

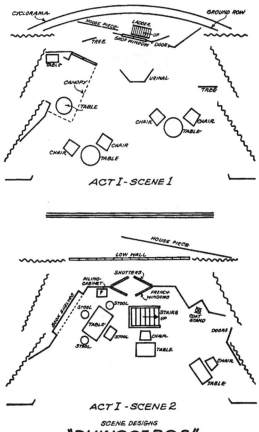

ACT I - SCENE 1

ACT I - SCENE 2

SCENE DESIGNS
"RHINOCEROS"

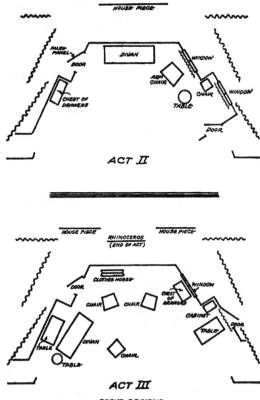

ACT II

ACT III

SCENE DESIGNS
"RHINOCEROS"

CPSIA information can be obtained
at www.ICGtesting.com
Printed in the USA
LVHW081109151122
733052LV00004B/317